FAITH *of a* FARMER'

God, Family and Life in
America's Heartland

To my friends at
Ivy Tech
Bryan Dee Kirkpatrick

BRYAN DEE KIRKPATRICK

Faith of a Farmer: God, Family and Life in America's Heartland

by Bryan Dee Kirkpatrick

Trade paperback ISBN: 978-1-943294-25-1
Ebook ISBN: 978-1-943294-26-8

Cover design by Martijn van Tilborgh

Faith of a Farmer is also available on Amazon Kindle, Barnes & Noble Nook and Apple iBooks.

Contents

Dedication

I dedicate this book to God the Father, Son and Holy Spirit, in whom I put my trust for my life.

Introduction

I HAVE ALWAYS WANTED TO WRITE a book about my life; first, so my wife, children and grandchildren would know what I was all about and second, in hopes that my story would help my children—and others—understand how God works in each of our lives.

When my children were younger, they sometimes expressed fear and anxiety about the future—friends, relationships, marriage, and so on. As you will read, I faced some of the same fears and experienced similar anxiety. However, I always told my children to put their trust in God and to ask Him to be with them, guide them, give them patience, wisdom and a clear feeling in their hearts that they are following Him.

This book is my story of doing just that.

CHAPTER 1

Beginnings

I WAS BORN OCTOBER 3, 1951, to Robert William and Wilda Ruth (Gentis) Kirkpatrick. I have one sister, Janet Sue (Kirkpatrick) Middlesworth, and she was born May 27, 1954. My father served in World War II fighting the Japanese—sometimes hand-to-hand. He was farming before he was drafted, and when he returned from the war, he ran a farm owned by the Leisure family in Grant County. This is where my parents lived when I was born.

Six weeks after I was born, they moved to Howard County to a farm belonging to Bruce and Frances Haycock. This was the beginning of the family farm.

My father's parents were Paul and Trela (Trobridge) Kirkpatrick. Grandpa died before I was born. My dad had an older sister, Ethel, and an older brother, Willis. Ethel's husband was Ernest Livezey, and they had two children, Charles Robert and Ruth Ann Livezey. Ruth Ann is living today. Willis was married to Pearl (Engleman) Kirkpatrick, who went by Pam. They had two boys, William (Bill) and James (Jim). Bill married Janet (Allen) and they have a boy and a girl, Allen and Brenda. Jim passed away in February 2012. Jim had three children, Chris, Craig and Carmen.

My mother had one brother, Rex Gentis. Rex married Maxine (Smith), and they have two boys. Gene has three children and currently lives in Kentucky with his wife, Becky. Phil and his wife, Jane, live near the family farm. Phil farms today and is one of my best friends.

FARM LIFE

My earliest memories are fuzzy, but I do recall that I was about four years old when my mother taught me the ABC's, how to count and how to say the Lord's Prayer. That was the last thing I wanted to do, though, preferring to be with Dad on the tractor or feeding the hogs and cattle.

Bryan at Grandma Trela's
at four years of age

Among the good things I learned from him, I picked up a few bad habits, too. I remember watching the Art Linkletter Show. I didn't like the timer clock used on the show, so I called it a bad name. My mother explained to me not to say those kinds of words, and I told her that Daddy used them. I don't exactly remember what all was said, but I do remember the feeling of Dad's belt across my behind.

I really enjoyed riding on the tractor with Dad. We would go to the Sims elevator to grind corn and bring back feed for the hogs. When I was about four years old, I was walking around the ear corn dump that went into a pit about seven feet deep with augers moving the corn. I slipped and fell, and a fellow by the name of Bur, who was working at the elevator, grabbed my arm, saving me from what could have been a terrible accident.

During this period of time, I remember one of my first times going to Bible school at Antioch Christian Church. The lesson was about Satan, and he was portrayed as a snake in a tree in the Garden of Eden. After the lesson I was so scared of snakes, thinking that all snakes are Satan. My mother, sister and I went home after Bible school, and Dad wanted to teach me to mow the yard. However, when I stepped on a snake behind the mower, I let the mower go and started screaming, thinking the devil was coming after me. Later, they tried to explain to me that the snake was not Satan, just an innocent little garden snake. I didn't buy their story, and I still don't like snakes of any kind today.

I often went to Swayzee with my mother, and she would always get me a five-cent Coke at the Rexall Drug Store. One day I was sitting on the bar stool spinning round and round. Mom told me to stop spinning, and about that time I fell off and cut my head open on my left temple. Doc King's office was across the street, and away we went. Doc said the gash was in a bad spot, and he gave me three shots in my temple and proceeded to sew me up. I think this is the first time I experienced severe pain that wasn't felt on my bottom.

At age four or five I remember being able to go to Grandma Trela's to spend the night—always an enjoyable experience. When I spent the night, we ate pancakes and bacon for breakfast. She made the best pancakes—I have never had any pancakes like Grandma's. Then we would go to the creek to fish, clean our catch and have fresh catfish for lunch or supper.

She didn't have much, but she had it all when it came to kindness and caring. Grandma had about 22 tillable acres on State Road 26 and 1150 East. My dad farmed the land, paid all the expenses and gave my grandmother the income. That is what Grandma lived on—along with her Social Security check. Grandma also had chickens and sold eggs, and she was known for using her rifle to kill the animals that ate the chickens.

Grandma called quite often for us to help get birds out of her house. One day she called, and there was a skunk in her crawl space. In an attempt to get the skunk out, we put mothballs in the crawl space. That was a big mistake. It smelled so bad that I had to go back into the crawl space to retrieve as many as I could, since I was the only one small enough to get in there. I never saw the skunk, but between the smell of the skunk and the mothballs, I stank awful when I came out.

Bryan and Janet, August 1958

We made many great memories at Grandma Trela's house. My sister and I loved to spend the night there. In the early years Grandma took care of her mother, Great Grandma Raines. Dad said we had a relative who'd married Chief Kokomo's daughter, and if so I'm sure it had to be through Grandma Raines's side. She was a cranky and demanding old lady, but now I realize that she must have had dementia and was just kind of bullheaded.

I remember going to Great Grandpa (Oscar) and Grandma (Minnie) Gentis's for Christmas. The Gentises had a larger family than my dad's family. My cousins Gene, Phil and Gary were always at the get together as well. Grandma and Grandpa Gentis were very conservative. She didn't like to spend money because of how difficult it had been during the Depression, and she was known for hiding her egg money. When we had a family dinner at Grandma and Grandpa Gentis's, it was always great to play ball with Gene and Phil. However, going to the Gentis side of the family—except for Gene and Phil—was just not the same great time as going to Grandma Trela's.

When I was about five years old, I remember driving the WD 45 through the gates for my dad. The clutch and the brake were too far away for me to reach, but the hand clutch was manageable. If I had ever needed to push the brake to stop the roll, it would have been difficult. After we got through the gate, we sometimes ended up at the corn crib. Dad would say we needed to throw out a certain number of ears for each sow, and I learned how to count by tossing those ears of corn.

I often rode my bicycle down to feed the feeder calves, the cows and the bull. Once at the corn crib, I had to throw out a certain number of ears for each of the groups of cattle. One day, right after lunch, I rode my bicycle down to feed the cows, climbed the rails into the corn and went to the corner of the crib. As I stepped into the crib, I also stepped in a hornets' nest and was stung all over my body.

I had hornets in my pants, my shirt, my ears and my shoes. I was screaming bloody murder, and Red Holmes, my dad's hired man, heard me clear up to the house. He came to the field as fast as he could. I had worked my way off the corn crib and was crying so hard that the cows were looking at me. Red picked me up and told me to hold my breath and not to be afraid. He put me in the water tank and held me down in order to drown the hornets.

Red then made mud balls and put them on every place I was stung. When my dad came to the field, they brought me to the house and took me to Dr. Beck. He had a nurse and receptionist named Janice, and I remember her being very pretty. They put me on Doc's table, and Janice called for Doc Beck to come in immediately. He gave me a shot and said he thought I would be OK, but if I got worse, they were to take me to the hospital.

When I was about this same age or a little younger, I remember my dad combining beans with a combine. I would take my shoes off, and Red would tie them up on the pipe that held the headlights. When the wagon was full, we took the beans to the Sims elevator and unloaded them into the same pit that I had almost fallen into a few months earlier. Dad usually got me a candy bar at the elevator, and we would split a Coke.

CHAPTER 2

School Days

1957-1958: FIRST GRADE

WHEN I WAS FIVE YEARS OLD, since my birthday was October 3, the big discussion was whether or not to let me go to school or to wait until the next year. One day Mom said that we were going to go see Mrs. Beeler, the first grade teacher at Union.

I remember sitting at her dining room table in the afternoon. Mrs. Beeler got a sheet of paper and a big pencil. She asked me to draw a straight line, a circle and a box. I did it well, and she then asked me to count to ten. That was a breeze so she had me say the ABC's. Then she asked me to write the first ten letters in the alphabet. She quickly learned that I could count and recite my ABC's, but I could not write them. I remember very distinctly that Mrs. Beeler said, "He will be just fine starting the first grade." She was so kind.

Stub McGraw was the bus driver the first time I got on the bus. He had a cigar in his mouth just like my dad, so I knew I would be in good hands. Then there were two very pretty girls, Charlene Smith and Kathy Wilkerson, who asked me to come and sit between them. They said they would make sure I got to the right places at Union. That started a very long-lasting seating arrangement for me. It was good too, because they kept me from running around and getting into trouble.

The first time that Charlene and Kathy were not on the bus, I was lost. I made new friends but found myself in trouble. The older guys picked on me, and I got in trouble for turning around and telling them to stop. One day when I got off the bus, I told Mr. McGraw what was going on and that I did not want to get into trouble because, if my dad found out, I would get the belt.

"Bryan," he replied, "I have known your parents for a long time. You work with me, and I will take care of you."

When I first got to school, I noticed the ABC's and the numbers on the wall above the blackboard. I was assigned a seat, and it didn't take long for me to get up and try to walk out. Mrs. Beeler explained to me that I had to sit in my chair and listen to her so I could practice what she was teaching us. I told her that I really didn't need to be there because my dad could teach me all this on the farm. That led to a discussion with Mrs. Beeler and my parents. The moment I heard the word "belt" my mind was changed.

It took some time to get used to the lunch at school. My mother was a good cook and always had very good food for us to eat. The same couldn't be said for school lunch, and we had to have another meeting with my mother and the teacher. What they didn't know is that I did not like creamed rice—one of the first foods I tasted at school. In fact, it made me throw up, which is what prompted the call to my mother.

"You need to taste a little bit at a time," Dad said, "and you'll learn to like it."

I never did learn to like creamed rice, but I did learn that the other foods they fixed at school were pretty good.

First grade was a learning experience for me—I was the youngest person attending the school. I learned how to write and how to get along with others. Mrs. Beeler was the nicest teacher I ever had, and neither she nor her husband had any idea that the little first-grade farm boy would one day be working their farm when he got out of high school.

1958-1959: SECOND GRADE

This is when life really began. I had learned to listen in class so I could participate at recess, which is where I discovered my love for baseball, softball and basketball. I asked my dad for a bat, a glove and a basketball, and I got them for my seventh birthday. It didn't take me long to learn that baseball was for me. We lived for our ball games at recess. One day a boy named Dale used my bat. He struck out, got mad, slammed the bat on home plate and broke it. I wasn't very happy about that, but Dale was a lot older than me—and a big bully. He didn't care about my bat, which was now in two pieces, and my heart was broken as well. My friend Robin was upset as well, and he confronted Dale about it. I thought Dale was going beat both of us to death.

When I got home, I told my Dad. He calmed me down and explained that the bat could be replaced. I told him I could really hit the ball with that bat and that I may not be able to hit the ball the same way with a different bat. We went to town, and Dad got me a new bat. When we got home, he and I played baseball. He told me how to hold the bat with the trademark facing up, to line the bat up with the middle of the plate to get my distance and—most important—to keep my eyes on the ball.

"If you keep your eyes on the ball," he said, "you should never get hurt. But if you don't watch the ball all the way into the glove or until it hits the bat, that is when you can get hurt."

I no longer had a fear of being hurt, but could I hit the ball with this new bat? Sure enough, I smashed the balls.

"Let's just leave this new bat at home," Dad said. "Use the bats at school. It doesn't matter what bat you use, you will hit the ball."

I was allowed to take my basketball to school, where I could use it at recess and then take it home each evening. One morning it was very cold when I put my basketball in the room where we hung our coats. About an hour after getting to school we heard an explosion. The teacher had us leave the room and go to the hallway.

The principal and teacher discovered that the heat change had caused my basketball to explode. The teacher, Mrs. Shenk, explained to me what had happened, and I cried and cried. I finally got over it, and when I arrived at home, I told my parents what had happened. They laughed. I explained to them that it wasn't funny, but Dad said we would get a new basketball, and I began to feel much better.

Little League Baseball was available at the end of the second grade, but Dad told me I was too young to play but could do so next year. I took it pretty well. Since I had never been on an organized ball team, I didn't know what I was missing.

1959–1960: THIRD GRADE

Mrs. Winger was my third grade teacher. She and her husband, Herb, went to our church, which meant she told my parents everything that went on at school. My parents were always concerned about me starting school so young, and in third grade I talked when I shouldn't have and had a hard time staying in my seat. It seemed like I was always the one who got in trouble.

As the school year went on, I discovered I was pretty good at ciphering on the blackboard in our math contests. I was thrilled at recess because we were always planning the big ball game. We chose captains and then picked teams. We even let girls play. As the year went on, I thought I was doing really well. I loved playing softball and basketball. I was almost always one of the last three standing in the ciphering matches, but my citizenship grade dropped to C during the first six weeks of school.

The next Sunday at church, Mom and Dad talked to Mrs. Winger about my citizenship grade. Mrs. Winger's views and my views were not the same, so I had a meeting with the belt later that afternoon. When I went to school the following day, I asked Mrs. Winger why she thought I was so bad in school.

"You're not a bad boy," she said. "You just need to not talk so much when I am talking."

"Am I bad enough to deserve a whipping after church on Sunday?" I asked.

She did not respond to me.

I was extra careful not to talk when we were supposed to be quiet. I noticed that the girls were the worst when it came to talking, but I was the one who got in trouble. When you get into situations like I got into, it's something you don't forget.

When I was older, Mrs. Winger and her husband went on vacation and asked me to get their mail, feed the hogs and cats and check the house each day. When I went into the house, I discovered she had newspaper articles lying on the table—stories about our high school baseball games. I was mentioned in every article, and I realized then that she really did care for me.

The school year ended, and it was time for Little League signups. My dad promised that I could play that year, and he kept his word. When I went to the first practice, I was the smallest one there. The coach, Paul Myers, worked with me.

"If you stay with me," he said, "I will make you a ball player—and a good ball player."

He said we had a lot of work to do to get there, though, so Paul and Dad taught me how to throw, field and hit the ball. Paul came to the farm one evening after practice.

"Bob," he said, looking at Dad, "it is time to get tough. We need to get him to throw better. He is doing well, but I want him to throw rockets."

Paul said that I would make a great shortstop, but that's not what he needed.

"I need a catcher," he said. "If you can catch, you can play anywhere."

He promised to teach me so well that my motto would end up being, "No one steals second base."

Paul and I started playing catch. He threw the ball harder and harder, and my hand began to hurt. We stopped for a minute, and Paul said, "You know how we teach you to keep your eyes on the ball all the way into the glove?"

I nodded.

"You best keep your eye on the ball and catch it, or you will get hurt," he said.

He started throwing the ball even harder, and I was getting scared—and a little mad. So I reared back and fired that ball to him as hard as I could. He took his glove off, threw it into the air, came running to me and picked me up, giving me a big hug.

"I have been trying to get you to throw like that all evening," he said, smiling. "I knew you could do it, but sometimes it just takes a little practice and guidance to see what you can do and to build your confidence."

When we finished that evening, we were throwing under the farm night light.

At our next game, I played right field. When my turn came at bat, I smashed a line drive to right center field. This was the official beginning of my baseball career, and I loved it more than anything. Within the next couple of games, Paul and my dad worked with me on the techniques of catching, and I ended up being Paul's catcher for the rest of the year. Dad worked with me on bunting. Even on the morning of the championship, Dad had me in the front yard practicing. He explained how important bunting could be at the right time in a ball game.

We were at the big game, and our team was behind with bases loaded. It was my turn at bat, and I laid down the perfect bunt— without the coach giving the sign to bunt. Then all I could hear was Paul Myers yelling, "Run, run, run!" The next thing I noticed after getting to first base was the pile up of players at home, with the umpire and coaches standing near the plate arguing. Our runner had scored, and we had won the tournament.

"Don't you think that was a little gutsy laying down that bunt without me giving you the signal?" Paul asked me afterward.

I told him how Dad and I had been working on my bunting and explained that we were facing a really good pitcher, Joe Smith. So I thought I would try it. He picked me up, gave me a big hug and told me he loved me. What a great first year in Little League.

It was a great summer even though I had experienced one of my worst school years yet. I had a great baseball season—and that is all I cared about. I did learn to be extremely careful around Mrs. Winger for the rest of my years at Union.

It was about this time that my parents bought the Rary farm, which is where our home is today. During the summer I worked on the farm, feeding hogs and playing with my little sister. Mom and Dad met with my Uncle Willie and Aunt Pam at least once a week to play Pinochle. But later that year, Dad and Willie had a falling out. They didn't speak until after my sister's tragic accident.

It all happened when I was mowing the yard, and Janet wanted to ride with me. I told her it was too dangerous, so she went over and played in the sand box. She found a knife and was cutting a rope when the knife somehow ended up in her eye. Later on, the family was gathered at the hospital praying that she would be OK. When we were at our lowest, Uncle Willie and Aunt Pam showed up, and I saw Dad give Willie a hug. I thought this was a hell of a price for my sister to pay to bring peace back to the family, and it reminds me today that life is too short to live with grudges. It is best to assess each situation and do your best to get the issue resolved, regardless of who is at fault.

It seemed like a long time before we knew Janet would recover, but she did lose sight in her eye. She adapted well and started taking piano lessons and—a few years later—voice lessons.

1960–1961: FOURTH GRADE

That summer, baseball was better than ever, except for one game that I remember well. My dad was working on the farm and wasn't able to attend. Later on, we gathered at our neighbors the Bramels' home, and I immediately began telling Dad about the game.

"I hit three grand slam home runs and a triple with bases loaded!" I boasted.

I could tell Dad was upset, even though I was excited. When we got home, Dad said that bragging like that was not acceptable in front of the neighbors.

"Let your actions speak for you," he said. "If you tell everyone what good deeds you do, people will naturally think you are bragging, and that is one of the quickest ways to lose friends."

Later on in the summer Dad and I were driving into Greentown to my ball game. At the east edge of Greentown we saw a girl we knew walking along the side of the road. She waved to me, and I did nothing. Dad asked me if I had seen her waving, and I said I had. He asked why I didn't wave back. I told him it was because she was a girl. He explained to me how rude that was.

"She was being kind to you," he said, "and you most likely hurt her feelings."

Dad taught me to always be friendly to people. He said I didn't want to be known as a snob or a brat, reminding me to always be courteous, respectful and kind to all of my fellow men.

1961–1962: FIFTH GRADE

I had dreaded going into the fifth grade because Mrs. Kistler had a reputation for not allowing any fun in her class. It was all business. However, I did not find that to be true. She was a very serious teacher but also kind to all of us who did not cause trouble. If you were a troublemaker, it was bad news for you.

In the fall it was all football. In the winter it was basketball, and softball was in the spring. That is what most of us boys lived for.

We knew Mrs. Kistler meant business in the classroom, so we tried to be extra good so we wouldn't have to stay in at recess.

I really didn't like the history and health classes, but I enjoyed math because Dad had always told me I couldn't farm unless I was good in math. I thought the other classes were a waste of time—except for English, writing and spelling. I almost always got A's in those classes. I had still not taken a book home to study in my school career at this point.

Later in the year our history lesson was to memorize all the states and capitals. I didn't take it seriously. We worked on them several days in the classroom, and I didn't pay as much attention as I should have. We had a test at the end of the week, and I got a "D" or "F"—I don't remember which. When I got to school on Monday, Mrs. Kistler told me I was going to stay in from recess until I learned every state and capital. I don't remember how many recesses I missed, but when I took the test the second time I got a 100 percent. A "C" went in the grade book, and I paid more attention in class.

In addition to playing Pony League baseball, I did a lot of fishing that summer. After spending the day helping Dad clear land, I asked him if I could go fishing, and he said it was OK. He told me he would drive the tractor back to get me at the forks of the creek at the Rary place when it was time to go home. I had caught enough sunfish and catfish for supper, and I saw Dad coming, so I made one more cast. The line and bobber got caught in the trees on the other side so I decided to swim across the creek to get them. The next thing I knew I was under the water feeling like something was pulling on my legs. I was very scared, but I was able to get back to the bank. When Dad picked me up, he asked me why I was all wet. I told him. He told me to never pull a stunt like that again because the creek had a lot of quicksand in it and that it was the river's undertow that caused my legs to feel like someone was pulling on them. I never swam in a creek again by myself.

Another day in midsummer Dad was working at the Rary farm near our neighbors, the Bramels, and I rode my bicycle down with my ball glove and baseball just in case Mike and Ken were home. It just so happened some of the other neighbor boys came by, and the next thing we knew we had a big ball game planned. I went back to the Rary place and asked Dad if I could go down there and play ball. He said sure, but when I saw him leave, I was to come. Later on, when I saw Dad leave, I told everyone I had to go. One of the kids said she had talked to my dad and that he said it was OK for me to stay. When I got home, I got the worst belt beating of my life. I never trusted anyone who claimed my dad had said something was OK again—unless I heard it directly from him.

Not only was this a great baseball summer, but it was my first year of 4-H. Dad gave me two gilts and said that whatever little pigs they had would be mine—although I would have to give half the profits to Mrs. Haycock, just like he did. Participating in 4-H taught me how to calculate the cost of feed used each day. I basically had my first lesson in determining income over costs and profit thanks to my 4-H leaders and my dad.

CHAPTER 3

From Boy to Man

1962 – 1963 – SIXTH GRADE

SIXTH GRADE WAS THE YEAR I got a rude awakening and found out a little more about myself. All was going well until the end of the first grading period. I had two bad grades—in health and history—so I brought home my books to study. This was the first time I had ever done so, and I did not know how to study.

When my dad came into the house for the evening, my mother made me tell him about my report card. He wasn't very happy and asked why I hadn't brought books home to study. Up to this point, I had told him that I was doing well in school. He informed me that getting these bad grades was not acceptable and was deserving of the belt.

He was right, and I never forgot. In the second six weeks of my sixth-grade year, the F's in health and history turned to A's. That was a hard way to learn how to study, but it worked for the rest of my school days.

This is about the time in life that I accepted Jesus Christ as my personal Savior. I think the day was March 27 or 17, 1963—I wrote that date on the corkboard of our blackboard in the kitchen. I never got in trouble for that because I knew that Mom and Dad were happy about what had happened. Reverend Ewing was our pastor, and it was because of his wife that I accepted Jesus Christ. I was baptized, along with several of my church friends, in 1975.

After making it through the sixth grade, some of us in Pony League got to play Lions baseball. We traveled and played teams in different towns. I most generally played shortstop. I caught some as well. I remember a game at Fairmount in which I hit one out of the park and broke the picture window of the people living across the street. I didn't find out until after the game. These were great times in my life.

1963–1964: SEVENTH GRADE

I found out very quickly that, as far as the classroom goes, junior high was a piece of cake compared to earlier grades. I enjoyed all the classes, and I knew what was expected of me so I could play sports. We had to go in and get fitted for our football uniforms, but practice didn't start until school started. I was slated as the second string quarterback from the beginning. I ended up playing on the defensive backfield and backup quarterback until I broke my ankle at my birthday party on October 3rd.

It was a big party, and all the guys were there. We were playing tackle football, and I stepped in an old stump hole after catching a pass and was then tackled. I limped around for about an hour and then Mom took me to the ER. My ankle hurt really badly for three days. Then it started itching. I was worried about basketball and concerned that I wouldn't be healed in time for tryouts. Coach Callaway saved me a spot on the team, and I got to play in about half the games at the end of the season. However, I had a limp that just wouldn't go away, and my dad almost made me quit. I talked him out of it, which makes me think it was really Mom who was worried about my limping.

I was usually the first one on the gym floor for PE class, and one day I started climbing one of the ropes in the gym. I got to the top and decided that I would go up to the steel rafters. I walked on the rafters about a quarter of the way across the gym until Coach Callaway, who was also our gym teacher, came out of his office and saw me. He pointed back over to where the rope was, and I knew that meant I had to come down.

"Let's go to my office," he said. "What do you think you are doing up there?"

"I just wanted to prove to myself that I could climb up there," I replied, "and after I found how easy it was to get on the rafters, I just kept going."

"Don't you think that is kind of dangerous?" he asked.

"No."

"Are you trying to get me fired?" he asked.

"Oh, no, Coach," I replied. "I'm very sorry. I won't do it again unless you give me permission."

"Don't worry, I won't give you permission," he said. Then he added, patting me on the head, "You farm boys are all alike. Don't scare me again."

Summer arrived, and Lions baseball was in full swing. I worked on the farm during the day and then rode my bicycle into Greentown to meet the team to go to the games or practice. Sometimes it was as far as ten miles to get to practices and games, and I did this many times from the seventh grade until I was a junior in high school. My parents would always be there to take me home.

1964–1965: EIGHTH GRADE

In eighth grade, my teacher was Mrs. Lamb. I remember one day we were discussing pronouns. She asked for us to name pronouns. I raised my hand.

"He, she, it," I said, not realizing how quickly I was saying the last two words. Mrs. Lamb didn't hear the pronouns; she heard profanity. So she sent me to the hallway, telling me to stay there.

The principal, Mr. Echelbarger, saw me in the hallway and asked why I was there. I told him what had happened.

"It just came out," I explained. "They're all pronouns."

He agreed with me and started laughing—I had never seen Mr. Echelbarger laugh before. Mrs. Lamb met us in the hallway in a rage, but Mr. Echelbarger told her that he had taken care of this matter and that it would never happen again.

About two weeks into the school year, I had a dream that changed my life in some ways. I dreamt that I was in a bar and someone attacked me. I slugged him, and he fell backward. I immediately jumped after him, and when I woke up, my head was sticking out the broken window of my room. When I had slugged the man in my dream, I was actually sleepwalking and had smashed the window next to my bed, badly cutting my wrist. The blood was coming out of my wrist and hitting the ceiling and wall. That's when I started screaming for help.

My parents heard the noise of the window break, and came into my room. They immediately got a handkerchief, tied it tightly around my arm and rushed me to the hospital. On the way to the hospital I told my parents that the hanky was too tight and hurting my arm. I managed to loosen it a little, and more blood started running out. Needless to say, they tightened it back up, and I was told to leave it alone. Dr. Beck was on duty that night at the Marion General Hospital. He asked me if I was trying to kill myself. I said no. He asked what I had been doing to cut my wrist so deep. I told him the whole story.

"Is he making this up?" he asked, looking at my parents.

"You cut the main vein in your wrist," Doc said. "I have sewn it up the best I can, but I can't promise you will have feeling in your right hand. I'm sure you have damaged the nerves in your wrist. You might get your feeling back in two weeks, two days, two months or never."

When the numbness wore off, I could tell my right thumb, index finger, middle finger, and the inside of my right ring finger did not have the feeling they should have. When I would pinch my thumb and fingers together, I couldn't tell if I had a dime, nickel or a quarter between them. I had about 50 to 70 percent feeling in my thumb and fingers, but in about two weeks I got used to it. It never changed, and I sometimes drop things in my right hand even today. I was fortunate because I still had enough feeling to throw a baseball, shoot a basketball and catch a football.

Of course, we were in the middle of football season, and this accident pretty much ended my days of quarterbacking. I only missed about a week of serious contact in football practice, but my hand had to be wrapped to protect my wrist. I tried not to use my right hand too much for tackling after the accident, and it all worked out.

On Palm Sunday, a huge tornado hit Greentown. It destroyed our high school and the southern part of Greentown, and several people were killed. I remember that earlier that afternoon I had asked Dad if I could take my rifle and go down to the creek to hunt muskrats. (This is the same creek that I played cowboys and Indians near as a much younger boy.) It was really warm out, and the wind was blowing so hard, it was all I could do to keep my hat on. Later in the evening, it started getting dark so I went to the house. I told Mom and Dad they needed to look outside. They knew a storm was brewing but did not realize the magnitude of it.

We looked out the north picture window and saw Lester and Dea Swan's house had been hit by the tornado. A few minutes later we saw Merrill Keys' house explode and then Harold Jones' farm do the same. The fuel tanks at the Jones' house exploded in the largest fireball I'd ever seen. Clarence Lavengood, who farmed for Grandpa Gentis, left his home and turned south right into the tornado. I'm sure he had a wild ride. Unfortunately, he didn't live to tell the story.

This year my dad let me have a six-acre hog lot for my own crop. I had to plow it, work it, plant it, pay bills for seed and fertilizer, split the profit with Mrs. Haycock and have records good enough to explain every detail of what was done to those six acres—along with giving her half of the soybean income. I had gone with my dad to Mrs. Haycock for years when he would explain what was going on at the farm, including expenses and income. Each time my dad would tell me to listen, because one day I would have to do what he was doing. Well, this was my first time to be the farmer and explain the expenses to Mrs. Haycock. I had everything written down as my dad had taught me. We walked in the door, and I was very nervous. I'm sure Mrs. Haycock noticed. She took us to the kitchen and got us a Coke. Then she showed me her doll collection that was worth a lot of money. She explained where every doll came from, and by this time I had calmed down some.

"Now, let's get the business started," she said, and I explained to her all that had been done to that six acres.

"That is what I like the best," she said. "When you bring me bills to pay and give me some money for the grain at the same time— that is what I like the best."

She proceeded to tell me how pleased she was with me, but then she said we had another issue to talk about.

"You are a lazy talker," Mrs. Haycock explained, "and you should be more responsible when pronouncing your words."

I told her that I had to take speech class from the second to the sixth grades. Being a former English teacher, Mrs. Haycock said I just needed to pay more attention to how I pronounced my words. Then she gave me a big hug. As Dad and I went back to the farm, he told me to remember that day.

1965–1966: NINTH GRADE

Due to the tornado, a lot of portable classrooms had been brought in for the school year, and classes continued as normal. We had been working out for football two weeks before school started, which consisted of two-a-day workouts. The freshmen had to hold the dummies for the varsity and junior varsity players. The older guys would hit us pretty hard at times and just laugh, and we had to hold our own the best we could. This was the price to pay for being freshmen. With the most consecutive wins in the state, our school had a football tradition to uphold—and now I was a part of that team.

When we played freshman games at home, Coach Calloway was always on the sidelines. He pulled me over and said, "Would you like to try linebacker?" I said I would, and he told me what to do, and when and how to do it. He sent me in, and I had a blast. When I came to the sidelines, he told me that I had done a great job. He was a kind-hearted man and a great football mentor.

When football season was over, it was time for basketball—and it was also about this time that I started getting headaches. I asked some of my teachers if I could sit in the front of the room, and they moved me. I didn't tell them I couldn't see because I thought everyone saw the same way I did. In math class Mr. Bugg asked me to do the problem on the board. I told him that I couldn't tell what the problem was. He later told me and my parents that I needed to get my eyes tested. We went to Dr. Jewel, and sure enough, I needed glasses. I was near-sighted, which explained why I could do the work in the book, but not on the blackboard. The first basketball practice after getting glasses was like turning the lights on in a dark room for me. I could actually see the rim, and it wasn't a big blur. I do believe this helped my basketball game quite a bit.

1966-1967: TENTH GRADE

This football year was a bit different. Coach Calloway had resigned and was going to Arkansas to coach a college football team. The new coach's name was Twyman Patterson. He very quickly showed the same charisma as Coach Calloway. Coach Patterson's summer workouts were harder than Coach Calloway's. Being 14 years old, I did most of the workouts at home. I had marked a quarter mile on the road and kept track of how long it took me to run it. Most of my friends worked out on the track at the high school. Coach Patterson had me listed at tight end and defensive end. I was on the second unit to start the summer workouts. By the time the first game began in the 10th grade, I was promoted to the first unit at both positions.

At 14, I weighed 130 pounds, and I was more man than boy, but I had a lot of learning to do. If the coach wasn't pleased with our play, that Monday practice was really rough, with meat grinders, sprints and a lot of pursuit drills. Being an end, I had to run farther than anyone. We ends encouraged everyone to do well because we knew if they didn't we would suffer the most. If Coach Patterson had told any of us to run through a brick wall, we would have tried the best we could. That is how much we all respected Coach Patterson. That fall, I noticed that my name was never mentioned as a starter in the newspaper. I finally asked Coach Patterson, and he told me that he had turned the starters in before the season had begun, and he didn't know that I would be working that hard to earn those positions. He told me I would be better off if I didn't read the newspaper.

"You go out there on that field and continue to work hard as you have been," he said, "and just let your actions speak for you."

With football season over, it was time for basketball. A few games before the end of the season, I broke my ankle playing at Union. Shortly afterward, we were leaving the high school in the school buses. Crutches, my saxophone, and a book or two for studying lay next to me in the seat. As our bus pulled away, a big snowball come in through the window and splattered all over. Some kids on the sidewalk were throwing snowballs at the bus.

I turned around to see what was going on, and the bus driver yelled at me. A few seconds later, I was hit in the back of the head with a snowball packed around a rock that had been thrown from the back of the bus. I turned around and told them to quit, but the bus driver slammed on the brakes and kicked me off the bus. He said I was not getting away with throwing snowballs on his bus. I told him I hadn't, and some of my friends told him the same, but he didn't listen. He told me never to get on his bus again.

Lester Swan, my mother's cousin, was driving the bus behind us and had seen everything. He stopped and picked me up, and asked me why I got kicked off. I told him what had happened, and Lester told me he had seen everything and knew I hadn't thrown the snowball. He told me that if Dad had any questions he should call him. When Dad got home, I told him everything. Dad knows that I would not lie to him—particularly after the belt beating from staying at the Bramels' playing ball years earlier. I think he felt so bad after he had found out I had been telling the truth that I had earned his respect, and he knew from then on I was a truthful person.

Me receiving some awards in high school

With school out, I threw myself into farming, even while baseball season was in full swing. I think it was this year that I started sometimes batting left-handed. When batting right-handed, I had a tendency to swing too hard. If I had two strikes while batting right-handed, I switched to the left side of the plate. I don't ever remember striking out after I started using this method. Sometimes I started on the left side, and when I got two strikes, I switched to the right side. I had problems striking out from the right side of the plate. I should have just made myself a left-handed batter and only batted right-handed against left-handed pitchers.

1967-1968: ELEVENTH GRADE

I was in eleventh grade, and two-a-day football practices were in full swing. Working on the farm between practices meant walking and weeding bean fields. Usually it wasn't too bad, as long as I had plenty of water. The only exception was between the two-a-day football practices. It made for a long and tiresome day, and I didn't have time to get into trouble because if I wasn't practicing ball I was home working.

That season, we had some great games. We had a group of guys that believed in each other, and we believed in Coach Patterson and the other coaches. More importantly, Coach Patterson and his coaches believed in us. One of the biggest games was at Western, and we won that game 28 to 26, even though we were the underdog. As a result of winning that game, we were Mid-Indiana Conference co-winners.

Coach Patterson taught junior English, and most of us had him for our teacher. I respected him in the classroom as I did on the football field. I really liked all my teachers this year—that is until the first grading period was over. Mr. Durr had told me I was getting a B in chemistry. When I got my report card, the grade was a C. I had already told Dad I was getting a B, and he was pleased. I went to Mr. Durr and asked why I had gotten a C. He said I had a bad attitude. I told him that I had never had a bad attitude and had always behaved well in his class. He wouldn't listen.

This was my dad's first year on the school board, and my dad and Mr. Durr were in serious negotiations with the teachers' contracts. If I remember, striking was discussed. They had met after Mr. Durr had told me I was getting a B. I think I was a victim of circumstance. I earned B's the rest of the year, and I think that was only because I had gone to Principal Wise and told him what had happened. About two weeks later, if I remember correctly, they agreed to a contract.

That year I was fortunate again to make the varsity basketball team, and I got my driver's license about two weeks before our first game. I used my 4-H money and a loan from Dad to buy a 1966 burgundy Ford Mustang with a three-speed transmission. It was a really nice car. After a game right before Thanksgiving, my dad said that my cousin Gene and I could go to Kokomo, but I had to be home by 11 p.m. On our way home from Kokomo I ran into some seniors who were drag racing. Gene and I avoided them, but a few minutes later, Gene asked me a question and I looked at him to answer. The next thing I knew we were out in the field where the softball diamonds are today. It had been raining fairly hard, and the field was really muddy. Marshall Shrock was close by and there in no time. We called Dad, and, well, I didn't get a good reception. Gene went home, and Dad and I towed the car. It cost $1,800 to fix it, and I had to ride the bus to school. It was rough on the homefront after that, but Dad got over it, and things were back to normal in a few days. I made sure my grades were exceptionally good that next six weeks.

I decided not to run track that spring. Dad had just bought a 160-acre farm, and we were occupied tearing out fence, rolling up barbed wire and pulling post. It was a wet spring, and we worked in a lot of mud. I didn't think we were ever going to get that woods cleaned up. I know that my dad was very pleased that I didn't run track that year.

It was time for baseball season to start again, and this year was a little different. It was the first year for sectional baseball. We had a good team but just not as good as Western and Maconaquah. I don't remember how we did against Taylor and Northwestern that year, but I played center field and loved every moment of it. I remember running into a little hitting slump about midway through the season. I was doing so well right-handed I didn't go back to left-handed for about two games. I had not had a hit in at least two games and maybe 20 innings. I was afraid I would be benched, but Coach Mugg stayed with me, although he did move me down from fourth to sixth in the batting order. We had a game at North Miami, and I finally came out of the slump. Coach Mugg came in early and was kind enough to give me extra batting practice. All I needed to do was keep my eyes open, lead with the knob and not try to swing too hard. I thank him and my dad for helping me get past that slump.

I've discovered that some people are gifted with athletic talent, some are gifted and don't apply it, and then others are people like me who just have to work hard and practice. When a coach continues to help you, you know he still believes in you. So, the best way to respond is to work even harder and make our best better at whatever we do. When I went through that batting slump, I was so depressed that I was afraid I would lose my starting position in my senior year. I prayed that God would help me with my hitting, but I think God thought I needed to be humbled. I was humbled, but I have never questioned Him for that. I learned that every person is different, and we need to accept what God has given us.

"You can do anything that anyone else can do," Dad once told me. "You may not be able to do it as fast, you may not be as good, but you can do it. You must accept who you are and then do the best you can within your means."

The feeling of coming out of the hitting slump was like a new lease on life. My last year of high school baseball was over and now it was time to concentrate on football.

1968–1969: TWELFTH GRADE

It was the time in the summer that two-a-day football practices began. All of us football guys who had worked so hard were now together for our last high school football season. The practices were easier on those who had done the summer workouts, and when football season finally started, our team was expected to win the Mid-Indiana Conference.

Our first game was with Maconaquah, and in the first quarter Roger hit me on a pass play. I collected my balance and side stepped the referee, but the defensive player crushed the referee. I ran about 65 yards for a touchdown. The coach at Maconaquah complained that I used the referee for my blocker. That was the first of several offensive and defensive touchdowns for that year.

The next game was Northwestern. A few years ago, I found a newspaper article in some of my mother's papers that had been written before the big Eastern versus Northwestern game. It talked about the touchdowns that I had and the touchdowns that Joe Breisch had for Northwestern in the prior week. Joe became one of my best friends later in life.

In spite of the high expectations, we got beat at home. The next Monday practice was back to meat grinders and pursuit drills. It was worse than two-a-day practices. Coach said that we had not come to play and that this is what it was going to be like from now on. He expected to win the rest of the games.

We did go on to win the MIC that year, and I would like to thank all the coaches and players that I had a chance to play football with for those six years from seventh through twelfth grade, not to mention my family. My Uncle Willis and Aunt Pam watched every football game that I played in, from my sophomore year to the last game as a senior.

In January of 2015, I found a letter from Ball State University in a high school scrapbook my mother had put together. I don't remember ever seeing the letter before then, but it was an invitation for me to come to a home game and then talk about playing football for them. I don't think my parents withheld the letter from me, but it's possible I just don't remember getting it. Looking back now, I would have considered playing for Ball State just because I knew it was a good school.

At the end of basketball season I started thinking about what I was going to do after high school. My parents had been insisting that I go to college, but I knew I didn't want to go to college for six years to be a lawyer or an FBI agent, and all that was left was the farm. I felt that if I went to college, I would lose four years of farming. I had always thought that being the youngest person in my class would give me a head start in farming.

As time went on, I got a call from the football coach at Taylor University, asking me if I would consider doing summer school and practicing football all summer. While the offer was attractive,

I felt it would put me four years behind on farming. I called Coach Davenport from the counselor's office and told him how much I appreciated his offer, but I felt it was time for me to concentrate on getting started in farming. He understood, but my parents were not happy.

"You *will* go to college," they said. "We don't ever want you to say you didn't have the opportunity to go."

They explained that they had never had the opportunity, but I couldn't even imagine Dad in college.

"Lord, what do I do?" I prayed. "Show me the way and where you want me to fit in life."

I asked Him to guide me and direct me so I could get out of this jam and make the right choices for my future. I talked to my parents about going to Indiana Wesleyan University, and they thought that would be great. My plan was to be close to home and still work on the farm. I did not want to go to a school far away because I felt that it would hurt my chances of getting farmland— and getting that four-year head start. Soon after, I was accepted at Indiana Wesleyan, settling the issue with my parents.

The next and final episode of completing high school was graduation. My dad was on the school board and presented me with my diploma. That was a big deal for him, but I just wanted to get out of high school.

CHAPTER 4

Big Decisions

1969

WITH SCHOOL OVER AND THE CROPS planted, my parents insisted that I see a surgeon. I was born with an extra bone in the left side of my neck, and it bothered me a little when I touched it. The surgeon had every reason in the world why it should be removed. I wasn't too pleased to have the operation, but I didn't have a choice. A few days later I went in for surgery, and the surgeon removed a bone-like tumor. He didn't know that the tumor had more little bones attached to it that had grown into my neck and alongside my windpipe. When it was all finished, I didn't have all my feeling on the left side of my neck and up toward the left side of my mouth. When these types of things happen, you have to learn to live with them and make up your mind that you will beat the challenge and not let it beat you. God will help, and all you have to do is ask Him. I've found that you can be in constant contact with God by feelings and not necessarily using language.

It was time for college classes to start, and I was careful to attend all my classes the first week. Some professors gave us quizzes, and others had us write essays. After the second week, I had an A average in every class for which I was given a grade. However, in the second week I was sitting in my History of Civilization class, and the professor talked the entire time about how the Romans chased some tribe over the hills with their elephants. That was the back breaker for me. I decided I was going back to the farm and not wasting my time in these classes that had nothing to do with farming. So, I went back to school on Thursday and spent most of the time in the gym with some of the basketball players.

I had already decided that I was going to try to get my tuition money back. I attended a class or two before I went home that day, and I didn't have any classes the next day, Friday, so I asked to meet with the president. I had met him at some social functions so I knew I could talk to him. I told him how I felt, and he said that he hated to hear me say that I was quitting school.

"I guess you can take the boy off the farm," he said, "but you can't take the farm away from the boy."

The president explained that they could give me 80 percent of my money back and asked if I was OK with that. I was very appreciative, and he wished me the best on the farm. I felt a tremendous relief, but my parents still didn't know. When I told my mother, it did not go well. When I told Dad, he was a little hard on me, telling me I didn't give college a fair chance. I told him I wasn't going to give it a fair chance if I had to sit in a class learning how the Romans chased tribes over the hills with their elephants. He didn't say much.

"Don't you ever say you never had a chance to go to college," Mom said.

"You made the right choice," Dad said later on when we were in the barn. "Your mother wanted to go to college but couldn't. You did it the right way."

Not long after, we went to Curless Farm Equipment in Fairmount, and Bob Jarvis asked if I wanted to farm their family farm the next year. Later on, we were working in the woods at the Gross place with Dad's D6 caterpillar, and Mr. Beeler, my first grade teacher's husband, walked across the field and asked if I would like to farm his farm. He made it clear that it was his wife who insisted that I farm the land. I guessed I had made the right choice about college.

We finished the corn harvest and plowing, and Lamar Dean, who owned the elevator, wanted to know if I wanted to work for him until harvest was over. He said he would pay me a $1 per hour, and I could work all the hours that I wanted. My priority was to keep the grain dryer running at night. I slept on a cot and set the alarm for every hour to check the dryer. I fixed semi tires and loaded semis in the daytime and watched the dryer at night. I got two or three hours of sleep a night, and Mom and Dad were concerned that I wasn't getting enough rest. When winter came, I worked at Accurate Parts until April 1970, when it came time for planting crops.

1970

We attended to the crop that summer, and I played fast-pitch softball. I had looked around, but I wasn't really dating anyone special. I decided that I was going to wait for the right girl to come along for me. I had talks with God about this situation, but I knew I just needed to be patient. Patience is not one of my best strengths, but I adapted, believed and had faith that He would not let me down.

Dad and I had worked deals with Bob Curless, the International Harvester Dealer, and I ended up with an IH 1456 tractor and Dad with an IH 1456 tractor with a cab. I also had an International pickup truck. In July International Harvester came to our farm to take a picture for the front cover of their magazine. We had the tractors, the pickup, dad's farm desk and dog in the yard for the picture. The IH 1456 without the cab was my first tractor.

Dad and I had several planning conversations regarding the best way to do certain jobs or projects. I was not bashful when it came to sharing my opinion.

"You are the most independent person I have ever known," he said one day. He intended it as a compliment because he knew

I never followed the crowd. I always tried to do what was right, even if it meant going alone.

The photo of Dad and me that appeared on the cover of
International Harvester's magazine

One weekend during the IU Football season, Denny invited a few of us back home to visit them at IU. I don't remember if we went to the football game, but I do remember the party afterward. I was just barely 18, and there was more booze at that party than I had ever seen in my life. Denny saw some people smoking marijuana, so he got all of us rounded up and suggested we get out of there. As we were pulling out, the police were coming in with squad cars and people carriers. Later we found out that some of the neighbors in the community had called the police about the noise. I never found out what happened after they arrived. I was just glad we were out of there when they did arrive.

One evening during high school basketball season, I was at Kevin's playing pool with the guys and Murel came by. He wanted me to go with them bush whacking. (Bush whacking was a term used for disturbing males and females who were parked in the country making out.) I told them I didn't want to go. They said one of the guys was going to jump on top of one of the cars. I went with them, but I really thought they were kidding.

Murel drove out through the country and stopped the car. Danny jumped out of the car, and we heard a loud thump. Danny had taken a large step and jumped on the trunk of the car, but we never heard the next step. The car had started, the lights had come on, and the next thing we saw was Danny jumping the fence, running to hide in the standing corn. The car chased us for about eight miles. When we were sure we had lost the car, we went back to get Danny. He had blood on his pants, and they were ripped from the barbed wire strand on the top of the fence—and he was scared to death.

"It sure took you guys long enough to get here," he said.

Danny then explained that the car he had jumped on was a convertible. He had fallen through the roof, and the guy had grabbed his leg, but Danny had kicked him with his other leg to get free. When we got back to Kevin's house, we had a story to tell—a story so off the wall that it took Danny's ripped pants and bloody leg to prove it. We didn't know that would be one of our last times together as the good old gang.

Our conversation later that evening turned to the draft and the Vietnam War. Murel, Roger, Judd, Gary and Ted drew low numbers in the draft lottery, but my number was 132. Later on that year each of them reported for duty. I don't remember whether I drew my number that same year or later, because I was younger than they were. What I do know is that while those guys were in the service, I prayed for their safety every day. And they aren't the only ones I prayed for during that era. I wanted to do my part, but I didn't want to lose the farm ground that I had picked up. Around March Tom Dickover came down and asked if we wanted to farm their place because he couldn't drive a truck seven days a week and farm. By the end of the year, I was farming nearly 500 acres.

CHAPTER 5

God and Country

1971

IN JANUARY AND FEBRUARY 1971 I took agriculture courses at Purdue University with my cousin, Phil. We made a lot of good friends, and I enjoyed learning something that would actually help me on the farm. We would come home all fired up about farming, but the whole time, in the back of my mind, I was wondering if I would get drafted. Dad had told me that he would do his best to keep the land if I got drafted.

A few weeks later I ran into some friends who were in the same situation. They had joined the National Guard and suggested I do the same. There was an opening for me, and I signed up. I was able to get the crop planted and scheduled an August sign-in date. I didn't have to go to basic training until harvest was over. I headed to Fort Leonard Wood for basic training in the late fall of 1971. While there, I quickly made friends with some of the fellow recruits—people from all walks of life. I found that basic training was like PE, but the people in charge were a lot meaner. If someone fell behind or did something the drill sergeant didn't like, we all dropped for push-ups. This is the way it was all through basic, but Sergeant Maddox, our drill sergeant, turned out to be a nice fellow after about two weeks.

We had classroom training some days or marched to the range, but we started every day with calisthenics. Everyone also had special duties every few days. My first time on kitchen police, KP, I worked every line before they put me on washing big pans. Hours later, a colonel came in the mess hall and back to where I was. I pulled my hands out of the water, and my fingers were bleeding. He saw the blood and yelled for the mess hall sergeant. When asked why I was washing dishes with bloody hands, the sergeant told him he didn't know about it. The colonel asked me how long I had been there, and I told him 19 hours. He ordered the sergeant to get me cleaned up, give me some bandages, release me from KP for the day, and to be in his office at 0800. The next time I had KP, I did nothing but wipe and clean tables.

We spent a lot of time at the range learning to shoot the M16 and the M60 machine gun. Sometimes they took us to the range on buses, but we always had to march back. When we were to the water tower about a quarter of a mile from the edge of the base, the sergeant would turn us loose. I was always the first one to the tower.

I was selected to go to St. Louis for the weekend for USO services. Many professional military were going to be there, and I was to represent the people who were currently in basic training. A few days before the event, we were marching back from the range, and a guy behind me named Luse hit me in the back of my head with the butt of his M16 and prodded me with his bayonet. I didn't do anything, and he pushed me out of formation, causing the drill sergeant from the other platoon to chew me out. I tried to tell him what happened, but in the Army you don't talk unless you are talked to.

I told Luse not to touch me again, but he kicked my foot and caused me to trip. I couldn't believe that Drill Sergeant Freeman wasn't going to intervene. Luse took the butt of his M16 and hit me on my ear while we were marching. Drill Sergeant Freeman wasn't around, and I warned Luse one last time. As we were making a right turn, he shoved me out of formation again. I turned around and slugged him, breaking his nose and knocking him out. He was out cold, and everyone marched around him.

We finally made it to the building where we turned our M16s in. I kept waiting for my name to be called—but not to turn in my M16. We waited at least 45 minutes while our superiors inquired about Luse. No one would talk, and I went forward. I told them that I would tell them, but they had to promise to listen to both sides of what happened. They took my M16, and I followed them to a room in the weapons building where Drill Sergeant Maddox waited. He let me have it. He said it was his platoon, and he wanted to know what was going on. He told me that he had recommended me to go to St. Louis, had given me some of the highest compliments of any person in basic training that he had ever led, and I was in danger of not going. I told him the entire story. He told me he saw what was happening but thought I had the situation under control. He apologized and said that if my story checked out with the other troops, he would support me the best he could.

We ran into the sergeant major and Captain Gray. Both were livid. I was left with the sergeant major, and he asked me what on earth had caused me to slug Luse. I told him the whole story, but I said I didn't want to be considered a complainer or a rat. He understood but admonished me to report such behavior. Once Drill Sergeant Maddox and Captain Gray returned, our platoon was grounded to the barracks. I was assigned night security and commanded to report to the captain's office at 1630 hours the next day. Captain Gray spoke to everyone in our platoon, and they corroborated my story. He couldn't understand why the drill sergeant hadn't seen any of it. We later learned that it was the first march for Drill Sergeant Freeman with a basic training unit.

I was on night duty that night, and a fellow by the name of Landis took sick. I went in to check on him, and he kept getting worse. I went to Drill Sergeant Maddox and woke him up. He called the ambulance for Landis. Come to find out, his condition was very serious, and he rejoined our unit about the same time Luse got out of the hospital. That same night Captain Gray showed up about two in the morning. Landis had just been taken to the hospital, and the captain asked me, "Did you beat him up, too?"

Drill Sergeant Maddox proceeded to tell him what was going on, and Captain Gray explained how I had ruined his evening and taken him away from his children and that he couldn't sleep because of me. We went into a room that wasn't being used, and he said he didn't know what he was going to do with me.

The next morning, I arrived about 30 minutes early for my meeting with the captain.

"Kirkpatrick, get in here," the captain commanded in a stern voice after opening the door to his office.

I thought I was going to the brig, but I went in and saluted as I had been told to do. He stood up and saluted back and told me to stand at parade rest and to not even think of moving. He sat back down, leaned back in his chair and started telling me everything that had happened with Luse, Kerry and the rest of the unit. He knew it all as I had told him, but more importantly as my fellow soldiers had told him. The captain said that it was not right for him to punish me or to strip me of the award I was going to receive in St. Louis. He said he hadn't had any sleep since the situation had come about.

"Kirkpatrick, I don't know why I like you like I do," he said, "but in some ways we need more soldiers like you. I don't want you or anyone else to think you can take matters into your own hands, but this is truly an exception."

His voice was not stern any longer, and he expressed that he wanted me to receive the award in St. Louis, but it couldn't happen. He would have to punish me somehow, so the other soldiers wouldn't think they could take matters into their own hands.

"This is the deal," he said. "You are to be at my office at 5:15 each evening for two weeks, and don't be late. You will not talk to anyone about our conversation or ever cause me any more trouble. If you do," he said, lifting his right foot above the top of his desk, "I will put a number nine spike on the bottom of my foot and run it up your ass. Do you understand me?"

"Yes, Sir," I replied.

"Then get the hell out of here," he said.

I went to his office every evening at 5:15. It was very cold outside, and the door was always locked, but I waited until 6 p.m. I about froze. Some of my friends would come and see me and bring me coffee from the mess hall. The very last day of my punishment Captain Gray met me and asked if I had been there every day. I said, "Yes, Sir."

"If you ever need a reference," he said, shaking my hand, "I will give you the very best."

I only saw Captain Gray a few times after this.

Luse got out of the hospital about three days after the incident. He came to me and apologized for the trouble he had caused. I told him that I hoped he was serious, and he explained that he had basically been a bully all his life and didn't realize how other people felt when he was making fun of them. He did change and was a decent friend from then on.

During basic training at the range, there were a lot of soldiers qualifying, as they were required to do. We would put three to five shells in our clips and then we would be given the command to fire. There were a few times I remember it being really quiet and then three to five rounds would go off in automatic mode.

Every time this happened, I knew that a soldier had received a "Dear John" letter from his girlfriend or, in some cases, his wife. These instances were hard to get over, and Drill Sergeant Maddox always reminded us that there was no girl worth taking your own life for. If you got one of these letters and needed help, he would see to it that you got the help you needed.

We were close to the end of basic training, and it was time to get qualified on the M16 rifle. That morning the drill sergeant told us to be sure to take our rain suits and parkas. When we got to the range, it was raining, sleeting and snowing. There was ice everywhere. The rain was freezing on our helmets and eyeglasses, and we could barely see the targets. Once we were in the prone position, it only took about 15 seconds for the sights on the M16s to ice over. This qualification determined whether we were to be considered an expert, sharpshooter or marksman. The scores were not good, so they increased the actual scores by 20 percent. The next few days we received training on grenades, and then we had to qualify throwing them. I was in the foxhole with a big fellow by the name of Rue. He had his grenade in his hand with the pin pulled and accidently dropped it at my feet. I picked it up and tossed it over the cement wall. It went off before it hit the ground. Luckily, no one was hurt, but my ears rang for several days after that.

We camped out every so often in the woods at Fort Leonard Wood. We were not given any prior notice. They could come in at 2 a.m. and tell us to load all of our gear and prepare to leave. One time they did this it was nearly 20 degrees below zero. When we went to bed that night, we each had our own very small tent. They told us to take off all our clothes except for underwear and T-shirt before going to sleep in our sleeping bags. Those who didn't do so got severe frost bite. The frost bite damage was mostly on the toes. I was glad to get back home for Christmas, but it was only for a few days and then back to Fort Leonard Wood.

1972

We finished basic training and went right into Advanced Individual Training (AIT). I was in the communications section, and it was a breeze compared to basic. I was one of four squad leaders. We had our own room upstairs. Richard Van Cleave, a fellow squad leader, became a good friend. There were about 40 in our platoon, and some of the guys were really rough and into pot. There was a young man by the name of Rea who was very young and the type you couldn't tell anything. Van Cleave and I had our hands full trying to keep him in order. Rea went upstairs and somehow got into the attic above our room. I was sitting on the side of my bed polishing my shoes, and the kid fell through the ceiling. I was covered with insulation and plasterboard, and his feet missed me by six inches. We gathered all the guys together and got the place cleaned up before the sergeant returned to march us to the mess hall. When Sergeant Mills arrived, he came straight upstairs to the squad leaders and prepared to tell us what to do to be ready for the next day. He told us to go down and assemble the troops outside, but he did not notice the ceiling. About two days later he asked how that hole had gotten there, but no one knew.

There was another instance with the guys who smoked pot. Six of them came upstairs one afternoon and started smoking pot all around my bed, blowing their smoke in my face. I pretended that I was asleep. I was scared and didn't know if I was going to get beat up or what. I heard someone coming up the stairs, and it was Van Cleave. I realized that we were getting ready to take on six other soldiers who weren't so friendly. A soldier by the name of Googe had heard what was going on. He came upstairs and told his brothers to get back downstairs and leave us alone. It was very tense for a while. Googe told them that Van Cleave and I were not going to try their pot and to respect our choice. If it weren't for Googe, I don't know what would have happened that day. I mentioned the situation to Sergeant Mills, and he told Van Cleave and me to not turn our backs on those fellows. He also said he would be around more.

The next day we started hand-to-hand combat training with a fighting stick that was a one and one-half inch dowel rod with padding on each end. We could only hit each other with the padded ends of the dowel rods. The fights began with about 200 soldiers and two rings. When it was all done, there was a fellow by the name of Snell who was about six feet and seven inches and I, who was about an even six feet tall. The drill instructor told us to go at it until we had a clear winner. Snell and I did go at it for a while, and then we started talking to each other about taking it easy on each other. When the drill instructor figured out what we were doing, he then ordered some of the remaining 200 soldiers to attack us two, three and four at a time. We finally went down, but not without a fight. I was exhausted and felt like I had been hit by a Mack truck. When we got up, Snell wanted to take on the drill instructor. The drill instructor refused. Neither Snell nor I liked him. And we never saw that drill instructor again.

AIT and basic training were about to come to an end, and I got papers that said I had to remain at Fort Leonard for an additional two weeks for riot control training. This was about the last week of AIT, and it was time to go camping again. It was fairly warm this time, and one of the troops had a visitor in his tent that night. It was a snake in his sleeping bag. He didn't get hurt, but it made several of us very nervous.

Before I had left for basic training, my dad told me about a farm for sale. He suggested using my cash from the previous farm year to buy that farm. I did and had signed the papers before leaving for basic training. While I was gone, Dad had torn the house down, cleared the orchard patch and demolished all the buildings to make the entire field farmable, except the woods. It was back to the farm full-time, with the exception of the weekend National Guard drills. We got the crops planted and had a normal summer on the farm.

CHAPTER 6

Love for a Lifetime

IT WAS ABOUT THIS TIME I BEGAN wondering if I would be married before I got out of the National Guard in 1977. I knew that God had provided for me to this point, and I had asked Him to show me the right girl. I knew He wouldn't let me down in finding her. It's natural to wonder what is ahead in life when it comes to getting the right job and finding the right companion. It is a lot easier to tell someone to be patient than it is to accept that yourself. This is where faith comes in. You must continue to be patient with God and trust Him.

With the crops planted and tended to, it was time for my sister to go to college. She had chosen Taylor University in Upland, Indiana. Instead of using a moving van to move her into the dorm, we used the tandem International Grain Truck. There were many students checking out the grain truck who had never seen one like that before. They liked it so much, they wanted to take a ride in it. I jokingly said I would be back on Halloween and give them a ride. When Halloween got close, my sister asked if we could use the truck for a hayride, and we did.

1973

The 1972 harvest was over, and the 1973 crop planting was just around the corner. We completed the planting season and had another good summer. One day during the harvest I was at Greentown Equipment, and my friend Steve said he wanted to fix me up with his sister-in-law. That was the week before Thanksgiving, and I had my first date with Susan on the Friday after Thanksgiving.

After meeting her parents, we were walking out of the living room to head out on our date, and something entered my mind as I was in the doorway between the living room and the kitchen. I was stunned for about two seconds as I saw in my mind a clear picture of Susan wearing a wedding dress. Then, as soon as it came, the flash was gone. We went to a hockey game in Fort Wayne, and that was the first date of many. We were engaged before Susan returned to classes the second semester and married August 24, 1974.

Susan was in college at Western Kentucky University, and needless to say I made several trips to see her. I took my clubs and played golf while she was in classes. When I picked her up at the dorm, it was quite an experience for me. The girls were all nice, but they listened to music very different from what I had ever heard. Susan and I had a lot of fun. I had a motorcycle, and she sat on the back of it as we would joyride around the country. I'm not sure her parents knew about the motorcycle rides, but Susan was a wonderful girl, and my prayers had been answered.

1974

When it came time for the wedding, I messed around on the farm and didn't worry about getting to the wedding until about 15 minutes before it was to start. I discovered I was supposed to have been there a lot sooner, but we still got married on time and left on our honeymoon. Susan and I went to Washington, D.C., and toured the Senate and House of Representatives buildings. We visited museums, and I remember that one of them had an experimental tractor that was run by a turbine engine. To my knowledge, it was one of the only tractors of that type ever made. There had been one on my dad's farm when I was younger.

We left D.C. and went to Ocean City, Maryland, where we went deep-sea fishing. Susan caught several fish, but I didn't catch any. We then headed back home through the Blue Ridge Mountains. They were beautiful, and we spent the night at the top of a mountain and both had lobster for the first time in our lives. The next day we headed back home to start our lives together in the real world. When we got back from our honeymoon, Susan and her mother made draperies, and she began helping on the farm. She even learned how to drive tractors and tandem grain trucks.

When we harvested in the fall of 1974, Susan hauled a lot of popcorn to TV Time in Kokomo. I had a brand new 1974 IH tandem grain truck that fall. Susan drove the truck to TV Time, and the fellows working there would dump it for her. We also hauled grain with a 1970 Chevy tandem grain truck and a 1966 IH International grain truck. It was the 1966 IH grain truck that I had loaded with corn to sell the previous December to pay for Susan's engagement ring. It took 550 bushels of corn to buy that ring.

Manville and Laura Conway were our neighbors when we lived at 11678 East 200 South, Howard County, Indiana. Several times Manville and Laura invited Susan and me to Florida with them for a week. Manville took us out to eat and introduced us to the horse and dog tracks. It was fun to watch the animals run, but one evening after the race we walked out, and about 20 people blocked the stairs. The women were crying and screaming at the men. We learned that the men had lost all their welfare money betting on races. I have had mixed emotions about dog tracks and horse racing ever since. It was a reminder that you must always make sure the needs of your family come before recreation.

We later made friends with Stan and Jan Conway who built a house at 1250 East 200 South. Stan was a nephew of Manville Conway. I remember Stan showing me their microwave oven when it first came out. He cooked some hotdogs in the microwave, and I thought they were so good. Stan and Jan had twin girls, and sometimes Susan and I would babysit them. I had no idea that I would be farming for those little twins today.

1975

Most people have read the *Footprints* poem. At the end, the poet describes how at first there were two sets of footprints in the sand, and then one set. This year is when I believe God carried me, like the man in the *Footprints* poem, when I couldn't walk on my own. I experienced more physical pain in 1975 than in all the other years in my life leading up to then.

I started planting corn on April 5th and planted a few acres that day. When the corn was being planted, we also used liquid fertilizer and a liquid insecticide call Furadan that was pumped to each row and put into the furrow for the seed to get a good start. That evening I got sick. I went to bed, and the next morning I was still not feeling that well, but I was able to work. Luckily, it had rained a little to keep us out of the field. I resumed planting on the morning of April 7th. The wind was blowing hard from the south, and I noticed that when I would plant traveling north I felt pretty good. When traveling south, I felt sick.

I did this all day and got a little sicker as each hour went by—I thought I was getting the flu. About 4 o'clock I was planting south and felt like I was going to faint. I stopped the tractor and turned it off. It took me nearly a half an hour to crawl to the truck. I got up on the back of the tailgate and didn't move. This is where Mom found me when she came to bring me supper. She took me to her house, and Susan came to take me home. Later that night Susan called the hospital. They figured out that I had been poisoned and told her to get me to the hospital as soon as possible. They also wanted to know the exact ingredients in the liquid Furadan. Dad went out to get a container and called the hospital to tell them.

When I arrived at the hospital, they put me on a table and started giving me injections. One of the injections was to help me with the pain. Another injection was an antidote to combat carbofuran, an ingredient in the Furadan. I was too sick to sleep, and I could hear the nurses and doctors talking about whether or not I would make it. I heard them say that they could only give me one more injection of the antidote. They gave it to me, and I woke up the next morning feeling better and went home. My dad went to the field the next day and found numerous dead birds on and around the planter. The fumes from the Furadan that had poisoned me had also killed the birds. Dad decided this product wasn't safe for humans to use, so he went to the company that sold the product and got it replaced with a granular insecticide.

Due to the rain, it was several days before we could plant again. While I was recovering at home, word had gotten out about what had happened to me. Representatives from the makers of Furadan showed up at our home and wanted to know how I felt. When they got ready to leave, they wanted me to sign some papers—agreements that I would not sue the makers of Furadan or anyone who sold it to me. Naively, I signed the papers. When I told Dad what I had done, he wasn't very happy. He believed that the people had come to my door just to make sure that I wouldn't sue them.

We finished our planting, and it was time to scout the fields to make sure the seeds were out of the ground and growing. I often scouted the fields on my motorcycle, and as I was returning home, I passed the Dickover home. I saw Tom's German shepherd come out from behind the trees running at full speed. I didn't think I could slow down in time to miss the dog, so I decided to try to outrun him.

The front wheel of the motorcycle hit the dog in the neck, killing it instantly and sending me flying through the air like Superman. All I could think of is that I would have to get into a curled position so that when I hit the ground I would roll. After flying at least 50 feet, I landed on the road. I hit my head, shoulders and rump and rolled in this order for at least three times. Amazingly, I ended up on my feet—or at least I was on my feet when I came to. I didn't know where I was. My glasses were gone, and I had so much blood on me that I couldn't see. I was rushed to Dr. Ridgeway's office and put on the table. The nurses worked to get the rocks out of me and to stop the bleeding. I could move my arms, fingers, legs, and neck, so I was pretty sure I didn't have any broken bones.

Doc proceeded to sew me up, and I ended up with stitches on my ears, face, nose and rump.

I am very thankful that I was given a second chance at life. In my heart, I felt God still had a lot planned for me on this earth, and this incident gave me a mental attitude to be more appreciative of what He had given me and—more importantly—not take Him for granted. I love the Lord with a more meaningful understanding, and I thank Him for sparing my life. I had not been wearing a helmet during the accident, and I'd been driving nearly 70 miles an hour. As a result, I was laid up for several days and could hardly move my arms. My elbows were so sore that Susan had to feed, wash and doctor me for several days. However, I did end up playing softball that summer.

When September came around, Dad and I decided to remove some slats from an old corn crib. I took the chain saw and cut the slats out for about three hours. I was nearly finished when I noticed a small slat I had missed. I fired up the chain saw and went to work on the last slat, but the saw kicked back, cutting my head open and slicing my nose. I saw pieces of skull in the chain and screamed for help. Dad brought a towel, and it was immediately saturated with blood. We got to my truck, where Mom had several towels, and wrapped up my head. It was decided that there wasn't time to call an ambulance, so Dad took me to Howard Regional. I was awake the whole way, and I saw blood all over the inside of the cab roof. Dad ran a few stoplights and kept talking to me to make sure I didn't slip into a coma.

When arriving at the hospital, there was a nurse who had one mission: to keep me awake. I don't think I ever did pass out, and I remember it took them a long time to sew up my head and nose. The surgeon was very kind, and he talked to me while he worked on me, telling me to stay awake. I'm not sure what he used to replace the skull, but he did say that there was enough skin to pull it tight, and he wouldn't need to do any skin grafting. The doctor told me that I was a very lucky man and that if the saw had gone into the skull another quarter of an inch, I may not have survived.

I told him that I wore glasses and that I had felt the chain lock into my glasses frame and kick back. He said that they had saved my life and remarked that I should never complain about having to wear them. Later on, when I went in to get the stitches out, he told me that I was his masterpiece.

As you can imagine, this was a very difficult year for Susan. She had been married a little over a year, had learned how to drive tractors, and had to nurse me back to health three times. We never did discuss the incidents too much. I am fortunate that, on each occasion, she was kind enough to take care of me until I was healed. This was the third life-threatening accident in six months. Make no mistake: I put my faith in God, and I am so thankful that He again gave me another chance at life. I have tried to do His will, and my goal in life has been to make my best better at whatever I do and help others do the same. This can only be done by being in touch with God and asking Him for His wisdom and guidance. This includes doing things that you wouldn't think possible. You must also meet every challenge and not let the tough challenges beat you. You've got to ask God to give you wisdom to make the right choices and for guidance to follow His path.

CHAPTER 7

Departures and Arrivals

O N JANUARY 10, 1976, VERNA (SWAN) GENTIS, my grandmother, passed away. Grandma Gentis was the first grandparent to pass in my lifetime. When life seems to be going along fine and then something like this happens, it is a shock that makes one realize the brevity of life. The sadness of losing a loved one is very difficult. We can say words of kindness, but that will not bring them back to this earth, and that is a major adjustment in life. If you believe in Jesus Christ as your personal Savior and have accepted Him, you have been promised a new life in Heaven. The scriptures have made it clear that there will be a life after death on earth in a place called Heaven. You can reach down deep and ask God to come into your heart and have that same promise of life after death, or you can be stubborn and rot like the opossums do on the highway.

When you get serious and ask Christ to come into your life, you will have an internal feeling within your heart that you will never forget. It will stay with you for the rest of your life. You must ask God to continually guide you, help you with wisdom and give you strength to make the right choices in life. I promise you the longer you wait to ask God to help you on any issue, the longer you will be in misery. If you haven't accepted Jesus Christ as your personal Savior, do it now.

When I was younger, I wondered where I would fit in life. I wondered where I would be farming. If I farmed in a certain geographic area, would I have relatives that I could call my roots to the area? I now know that I have family roots in this area where I farm. Christopher C. Kirkpatrick, who was the oldest brother of my great grandfather, George Washington Kirkpatrick, homesteaded land that I own today on the southwest corner of County Road 1400 East and State Road 26. Christopher was born in March 1844. The day I purchased the land that Christopher had homesteaded, my dad and I were late to the auction, but we were not too late to bid. They started the bidding as we sat down. I never saw the fellow who made the last bid before our bid. I bid the next time and then no one else bid. That is how we ended up with the farm. I have requested that my children and grandchildren keep this land out of respect for my parents and their forefathers and foremothers. If they use the income off of the land and allow future generations to do the same, I believe it will be a good investment forever.

1976

In 1976 we planted and harvested the crops without any accidents or major incidents, but we did have some exciting news this year: Susan was carrying our first child. The baby was due in December 1976. When we found this out, we kept it a secret until the bump began to show. Considering the events of the previous year, I had a lot to think about. So, soon after I found out Susan was pregnant, I had a quiet time with God in our living room. I thanked him for sparing my life in 1975, and I asked him to protect our child so that it would be healthy. I prayed that He would use this child to glorify His name.

Laura was born on December 1, 1976. Christmas came and went, and six weeks after Laura was born, we took off to see Manville and Laura Conway in Fort Lauderdale, Florida. We left home, and it was well below zero. When we got to Louisville, it was three degrees below zero. I don't think the grandparents were too thrilled about Susan and me taking our six-week-old daughter to Florida in this kind of weather, but we stayed a week before coming back home. During the planting season of 1977, Susan worked the farm with me. She took the baby seat and propped it up between her seat and the tractor cab wall. The spring and fall went well, and little Laura was the joy of life. Laura also rode along with me, and one evening she was with me while I was chiseling in the fall. I lost track of her in the cab, and when I found her, she had curled herself up on the floor with her head under the clutch. I picked her up and stopped the tractor. To this day, it gives me cold chills to think about what would have happened if I had depressed the clutch while she was there.

Laura would often ride with Mom in the cab
of the tractor.

CHAPTER 8

Close Calls

1977

M Y DAD AND I PUT IN A GRAIN LEG and pit to unload corn, extended some bins and built new ones and installed a new grain dryer. All the corn we harvested came to this location to be dried instead of moving the grain dryer from farm to farm. We had purchased enough tandem trucks to make this type of an operation work. We set a 60-foot auger to the bin or corn crib and then backed the truck up to the auger. The trucks had hoists on them, and we raised the truck beds until all the corn had come out of the truck. It took about 20 minutes to unload a truck that held about 600 bushels.

Dad and I traded our Gleaner L for a new state of the art TR 70 Combine. It was one of the first rotary threshing combines on the market. One day, I had finished harvesting soybeans south of State Road 26 and was taking the combine to the shop. I came up to a bridge, and there was a car coming from the east. I pulled over to the side of the road to let the car pass on the bridge. As soon as the car passed, I was hit very hard by a pickup truck, and the boat the pickup was towing flew up over the truck and hit the combine on the top edge of the grain bin, grazing the engine before hitting the grain tank. The impact of the boat lifted the back of the combine straight up in the air. Next thing I knew, I was in the cab looking down at the creek over the edge of the bridge. When I was able to get out of the combine, I checked on the two guys in the truck. They were OK but shaken, and when I talked to them, I smelled alcohol. I don't think we will ever know whether they were drinking and driving or if the impact burst their beer cans. The neighbors smelled the beer, but the police didn't check to see if alcohol was involved.

My dad was traveling north on County Road 1330 East about a mile north when he heard the crash, as loud as if it had taken place right next to him. About 25 neighbors showed up at the accident site to see if we needed help. We towed the combine off the road into a field with our farm tractor. The combine was totaled. We later discovered that an ax had flown out of the boat and cut an eight-inch gash through the metal in the grain tank about four inches above the sight window. In other words, if that ax had hit four inches lower, it would have smashed into my head.

Our insurance company worked with Greentown Equipment to make sure we had a new combine and grain platform to finish harvest. I thought everything had been taken care of when I received a letter in the mail about the time harvest was finished. The fellows who hit me in the combine were suing me. I couldn't believe it, and it was very difficult for me to accept. I had done nothing wrong but was being sued by these fellows after they ran into me with their truck. If I had been driving the old combine when they had hit me, they would have been decapitated.

About the end of 1977 and the beginning of 1978 our insurance company hired a new, young attorney in town named Tom Trauring to represent me. He called me to set up an appointment, and we discussed what had happened. The next thing I knew we were giving depositions, and the case that never should have been was now in high gear. The trial was set for summer. During the trial, the opposing attorney, Bill Beck, asked questions that were clearly meant to entrap me, but Mr. Trauring guided me when these types of questions were asked. It was just like *Perry Mason* in real life.

At one point in the trial, Mr. Beck accused me of not having lights on the combine. Mr. Trauring called Mrs. Carolyn Durr to the witness stand. Mr. Trauring asked if she had seen the combine turn onto State Road 26, and she said she did—with the combine "lit up like a Christmas tree." The trial should have been over at this point, but Mr. Beck brought up all sorts of issues to try to prove that I had done something wrong. We couldn't bring up the presence of booze in the truck because no one who had smelled it wanted to get involved.

At the end of the trial—before the jury had reached a verdict—Mr. Trauring said that Mr. Beck wanted to have lunch with my dad, Tom and me. I told Mr. Trauring that I did not want to have lunch with him because he had twisted the truth and lied throughout the trial. But Mr. Trauring and my father convinced me to have lunch with them and Mr. Beck. I remember sitting at the table. My dad was at my left, Mr. Trauring was across from me, and Mr. Beck was to my right. Mr. Trauring started telling me that I did nothing wrong and should have never been sued. Then Mr. Beck admitted, "Bryan, you did nothing wrong. I was on your side the entire trial. I want you to understand that I was being paid to defend my client to the best of my ability."

"If you knew I did nothing wrong, why did you twist the truth around on some of the questions you asked me while I was on the witness stand?" I asked.

He said that was part of his job and that the way I answered those questions proved my innocence that much more. In the end, I did learn to respect Mr. Beck, and the jury came back and said I had done nothing wrong. They ruled that my insurance was to pay for my loss and that the insurance of the fellows who sued me would have to pay for their loss.

CHAPTER 9

Exploring

1979

It was 1979, and Susan, Mom, Dad and I were really looking forward to the Beck's dealer trip to Las Vegas, Los Angeles and San Diego. About 100 people traveled with us, and the first stop was Las Vegas. I was amazed at the lights and how inexpensive the food was. I explored a bit with Lee Rulon, and did he know how to show us a good time! I remember my friend Russ turning a $10 bill into $1,700 in about an hour at the blackjack table. Next we all headed for the bus to tour the Hoover Dam. We learned the history of the dam and saw what seemed to be nearly every inch of it, but I was ready to go back and watch people at the blackjack table. Dad walked into Caesar's Palace and put five silver dollars into a machine and hit the jackpot. I started playing a little blackjack, but I didn't quit when I got ahead. I ended up giving it all back.

I was interested in the craps table, but I didn't know how to play. I walked up to a table, and Lee asked if I was going to play. I told him I didn't know how. He said to do what he did and that he would explain it to me as we went along. I think Lee and I both made around $500. Lucky for us, it was time to leave for dinner or we would have lost it all again.

The second leg of the trip was Los Angeles. We toured the area where movie stars lived and visited shops where the movie stars shopped. We then spent most of a day on a private tour of Hollywood. It was interesting to see how the sets were made for shows—the part you don't see at home on TV. We took buses to the third stop on the trip, San Diego. I thought it was the most beautiful place I had ever seen. Our group stayed in a high rise across from the naval station. We could see the big ships coming in and going out. Lee, Phil and I sat on the balcony about three floors from the top and talked farming.

In 1980, the Beck's dealer trip was to New Orleans during Mardi Gras. This year Tom Maple and Mark Maple went with us, along with several Beck's dealers. We all purchased cowboy hats, and I had oysters in the half shell at every meal. The parades were different than any parade I had ever seen, and the people on the floats threw out beads, necklaces and ornaments as they passed. Bourbon Street was different from any place I had ever been. Some of the people we saw would have been arrested in Greentown, Indiana, for public indecency. I remember Doris Smith saying, "Lord, please don't come now. You won't be able to find us."

1980

I had been thinking of running for the school board for about a year. As soon as I noticed in the Greentown Howard County News that Max S. was not going to run, I filed the paperwork on the first day of filing. Before long Max changed his mind and decided to run after all. I took this as a personal statement that he thought I wasn't qualified to sit on the school board, but it only gave me more drive to work harder to win the office. I did win and served the Eastern Howard School Board for the next 20 years.

During planting season that year, Susan and I found out we were expecting our second child. Andrea was born on September 13, 1980—a harvest season baby. She was screaming when she was born, and she screamed for several months afterward. Laura had been so quiet and hardly ever cried, but Andrea made up for her in the crying department. I was really concerned about Andrea crying so much, but people assured me it was normal for some infants. This same year my sister and her husband lost two children at birth. I felt so sad for them, but there was nothing I could do to bring those babies to life. It was all in God's hands. Life is sometimes like a graph, with ups and downs representing all the events that occur in our lives. With two little girls, Susan and I sometimes felt we were on the top of the graph, but there were situations that caused sadness as well—things in life that were not in our control. We learned that when events happened that made us sad, we had to learn to beat the challenge and not let the challenge beat us.

One of these challenges occurred on April 27, 1980, when my uncle Willis Washington Kirkpatrick was playing golf in Hartford City, Indiana. He was waiting his turn to putt and collapsed dead of a heart attack. He had made comments earlier that if he died on the golf course, you would know he died happy. Uncle Willie was the plant superintendent of Kingston Products in Kokomo, Indiana. I always dreamed that Willie would retire from Kingston and work with Dad and me on the farm, but it just wasn't meant to be. It doesn't hurt to dream and hope. Nothing can become a thing until it is once a thought. Not all thoughts become things, but the ones that do are very rewarding.

That same year, one of my landlords, Robert Haycock, passed away. I have always appreciated his kindness in letting me farm his farm the year after I got out of high school. He and his family were and still are very dear to my family.

Later that year, on December 2, we lost Grandpa Von Alton Gentis, who died at the age of 77. Grandpa would come to our house to visit Laura and Andrea about every two weeks. When Laura was just beginning to talk, Grandpa came to the door one day, and out of the blue Laura spoke up and said "pickle." She called Grandpa Gentis "Pickle" from that day on. Grandpa Gentis had preserved the old German family Bible that had been brought across the Atlantic from Europe sometime between 1795 and 1800. It had been published in 1775. Grandpa was a good man—albeit always serious. I remember one day when he was using a push weed mower around a tree. I came up behind him and scared him and earned myself a lecture.

Another time, when I was about 10 years old, Grandpa Gentis and I went fishing at a lake up north. When we came in from fishing, we were getting the boat close to the pier when Grandpa stood up in the boat to grab the post on the pier. The next thing I knew he was out of the boat and under the water. Luckily, the water was only about three feet deep. I thought Grandpa was never going to get his breath. I didn't think I'd done anything wrong, but yes, I got the blame for Grandpa falling out of the boat.

CHAPTER 10

Influencing the Community

MY FATHER, ROBERT KIRKPATRICK, had served on the school board for four years prior to Max S. being on the board for eight. As I mentioned earlier, my dad handed my sister and me our diplomas during graduation. This meant a lot to Dad. He enjoyed being on the school board but didn't like being tied down to meetings. We had some close friends who taught school and helped me get a better overall view of what was going on in the school system. The big issue when I ran was that the board had voted to put in an asphalt athletic track. I did not discuss the asphalt track during the election, but I did emphasize the importance of reading, math and science.

The board was responsible for the track, a new library and new classrooms. I went down every day to review the work that was being done. One day I noticed that a drainage tile on the east end of the football field didn't seem to be in the right place according to the architectural plans. I went to see Mr. DeWitt, the school superintendent, and told him what I saw. At first he ignored me, so I had to be a little more forceful to get his attention. We walked over to the football field, and I showed him what the contractors had done, but he wasn't sure I knew what I was talking about. I showed him the plans, and he admitted that what I found could be a problem. The main sewer line from the town was very close.

It was at that moment that I earned the respect of Mr. DeWitt. He asked me how I understood the plans so well. I told him I had taken shop in junior high and high school, and that was the kind of thing Mr. Callen and Mr. Mugg had taught me. Mr. DeWitt initially had a hard time accepting me on the school board. He remembered that, when he was the principal of Eastern, Union and Jackson, I was in the first grade.

"I cannot believe that I remember you from the first grade," he said, "and now you are my boss!"

The drainage deal with the track broke the ice for us. Up until that time, I had some pretty tough interaction with Mr. DeWitt and the other board members, but he became a very good person for me to work with. He would listen to my newer ideas, and it seemed like from that point on Mr. DeWitt and I teamed up against the rest of the board on one issue or another. Mr. DeWitt was a retired officer in the reserves and knew how to take control of business. He was a good man at heart, but sometimes, as superintendent of schools, he had to take stands that some people didn't like. Mr. DeWitt was successful because he trusted in the Lord. Sometimes we had conversations about trusting in God, and during my period on the school board, I often prayed to God on the way into the meetings and asked Him to give me the right words to say that would soften the hearts of some of the other board members, so we could be sure to make the right decisions in the best interest of the students.

I have performed chaplain's rites for the American Legion for many years. When Mr. DeWitt passed a few years later, I performed the chaplain's rites at his funeral. As I spoke, I shared that Mr. Dewitt had had excellent leadership skills and that because of his skills the community had been a great place to raise families and educate children. I noted that Mr. DeWitt's spiritual, educational and financial leadership made a tremendous impact on each of us and thanked him and his family for their contribution to our community. When the service had ended, Mrs. DeWitt came to me and told me how Mr. Dewitt had talked to her about me. She told me that if he had ever had a son, he would have wanted him to be like me. That brought tears to my eyes.

***

When I began serving on the school board, there were serious water leaks in many places where remodeling had been done. We had a meeting with the architect, the general contractor and the roofer. As we walked to the library, anyone could clearly see that the caulk used at the seams of the bricks and joints was not the proper kind. It was a cheap caulk that wouldn't expand with the weather. The general contractor agreed to replace it.

Then we went north to the new elementary wing where the water poured into the classrooms. There were flashing issues with the roof, but Mr. Mays from Mays Roofing told me I was "a damn little punk" and that I didn't know what I was talking about. He cussed me out for about four minutes, but I continued, telling him that I didn't think the flashing was the only issue. The parapet walls were not built properly, and when I pointed this out to him, Mr. Mays started cussing out the architect. I told all of them they had better start answering questions, or they would be answering them in court. The general contractor finally explained that they had been tired of covering up all the mistakes of the architect and had simply told the workers to build as the plans said. The flashing had been left out of the drawings, which is why the water poured into the classrooms.

I told him that, as the general contractor, it was his job to correct this type of issue. He told me that he had voiced his concerns to the architect, but no one listened. Therefore, it was built as the drawings had instructed. The school board sued the general contractor and the architect and ended up with enough money to repair the parapet walls. This time, we hired a different architect, Bob Taylor, to make sure the walls were rebuilt correctly. Bob was there almost every day, working as the architect and contractor.

***

75

Around 1982, we started looking at computers to purchase for the school. The only computer I had ever seen was the big one on the Purdue University campus. A company wanted to sell us computers, and the salesman was telling us how they would help in the education process. As I listened, it sounded like a dream come true to me. Students would be given problems to solve and then put the answers in and be told right away if they had the right ones. If they did not have the right answers, they were prompted to try again. Over the course of the years that followed, I lost count of how many computers we bought and upgraded for the school.

CHAPTER 11

Getting in the Game

1983-1986

ICONTINUED TO PLAY IN THE CHURCH softball league and in a league in Kokomo. At 31 years old, I still had the enthusiasm to play sports that I had as a boy. An avid Cubs fan, I listened to WGN radio regularly and seldom missed a Cubs game while I was working on the tractor. One day while I was listening, Randy Hundley was advertising his baseball camp in Scottsdale, Arizona. I had heard the ads several times throughout the summer, and around the end of October, I finally wrote the phone number down.

The farming year had not been going well. It was the driest year I had ever seen, and the rust in the water in our well kept getting harder and harder to control. The shower curtain was so rusty that Susan finally threw it out, and Laura and Andrea used it as a slip and slide on the dry, crunchy grass. Our water well went dry, and a new well had to be put in while we were on vacation. Susan was due with our third child in November. Jenna Blair Kirkpatrick arrived on November 25, 1983. The farm yields had been terrible, and making ends meet was strenuous. But being blessed with Jenna helped us overlook my worst crop in history.

We always tried to make a visit to see Mom and Dad in Bradenton, Florida, sometime in January, but this year I had planned my first trip to Randy Hundley's baseball camps. It worked out that our neighbors Stan and Robin went with Susan and me to Scottsdale, Arizona, to play with former Chicago Cubs. Laura, Andrea and Jenna went with us as well. Jenna was only four months old, and Stan and Robin brought their youngest boy. Susan was glad that Laura and Andrea were able to help with the little ones.

We had a great time playing with Fergie Jenkins, Glenn Beckert, Jose Cardenal, Billy Williams, Ron Santo, Don Kessinger, Jim Hickman, Gene Oliver, Paul Popovich, Phil Reagan, Joe Pepitone and Ernie Banks. Steve Stone made an appearance, as well as a few former players who wintered in the Scottsdale area. Stan and I enjoyed ourselves—and we did pretty well. If I remember correctly, I pulled a hamstring but refused not to play. The trainers wrapped my leg just like they did for the pros. In the big game on Saturday, I could hardly run, but I was able to play third base and bat. I hit a high infield fly to third base. I'm pretty sure Ron Santo dropped that ball on purpose so my children could see their daddy on base.

In addition to the baseball camp in Scottsdale, I also attended Randy's mini camp in Chicago each year. We practiced and played with the former pros in Wrigley Field. Former player Larry Bittner joined us one summer. It was a thrill to hit one ball off the 368-foot marker, but Larry hit about every pitch into the bleachers during practice.

"Country," Randy told me, "when you come to Arizona next year, I will teach you how to hit all pitches as if you were in the major leagues."

This year was also Laura's first year in Pixie Softball in our local summer league. Susan and I had been good friends with Ross and Linda Flodder, and one evening Ross asked me to help coach the Hasler Pickett softball team. This league was made up of girls 12 and younger. I had coached a Lions baseball team when I was just out of high school, but I was a little hesitant about helping

Ross coach girls. After the second Lions baseball game in 1969, I'd got a little firm in practice. My rule was if you stood at the plate and watched strike three go by without swinging, you had to run around the football field passing by each goal post and back to the starting point as fast as you could.

There had been about three players I told to make that run, and the next batter was a boy named Doug. He watched the third strike fly over the plate, and I told him to make the circuit around the football field, but he refused. In not one of my finest moments, I grabbed his shirt with both hands and told him he had great potential, but he was letting it go to waste because he was too lazy.

"If you want to play on my team," I told him, "you will do what I say, and you should be a leader for the rest of the team."

He took off running around the football field, and when I looked down, I saw I had some of his shirt in my hands. I felt really bad, so I stopped practice, and we all watched Doug run. I told the team that Doug had decided to be a leader and that each of them could be leaders as well. I then asked Doug if he would like to bat again. He said he would. Doug went to the plate, and I threw a few pitches to him. I threw a changeup, and he fouled it. Then I threw a curve ball, and he swung and missed. The next pitch I threw as hard as I could—wanting him to strike out swinging. The ball was a little outside, and he swung and smashed that ball. It would have been a home run, and I met him at the plate and gave him a big hug. I was so happy. I called practice for the day and spent the next 30 minutes talking about what had happened and what each of them could do when they put their minds to it. Everyone left on a high note, but my problems had just begun.

Doug's mom called me at home wanting to know what had happened at practice. I knew his mother pretty well, and I got to know her even better—but not in a good way at first. I told her I would meet her at the ball diamond parking lot. We met, and I explained my philosophy and apologized—not for the way I taught but for grabbing Doug's shirt.

"Bryan, I appreciate you trying to make my boys the best they can be," she said, giving me a hug. "However, the next mother may not be so understanding."

I had a discussion with the team about the shirt. I told them I would not change the way I taught and that I expected them to do the best they could at whatever they did in life. Doug's mother was there, and as the boys took the field for practice, she gave me another hug, and I gave her enough money to buy Doug and his brother two shirts each.

This is the story I told Ross when he asked me to coach the Pixie softball league. I told him I would treat the girls the same way I treated the boys, except no torn shirts. He just laughed. This was Laura's first year in Pixie, and we had a great year with a great group of kids. I remember telling the parents, "If your daughter is here for a picnic, then I suggest going to another team." That wasn't necessary, because we ended up having one of the best teams in the league. It didn't take long for me to earn respect from all the parents who didn't know me, and it was a thrill to see Laura and every other player when they got their first hits.

When our season was over, I was asked to coach the 10 and under all-star team. We sponsored a tournament and won several tournaments as well. By the end of the season, everyone knew my theme was "my way or the highway." However, in my 12 years of coaching Pixie league, I only had one girl take the highway. She was one of the most talented players, but she thought she knew it all, and her mother was the most closed-minded, self-righteous woman I have ever met. When the other players saw what happened, they supported me. The team went on to win tournaments without the star player and the all-star mother.

1985 was a great year for play in Randy's baseball camp. It was a mixed camp with the Cardinals, including Bob Gibson, Joe Cunningham and Al Hrabosky, also known as the Mad Hungarian. As he had promised, Randy worked with me on my batting, and it didn't take long for me to start hitting balls out of the park in practice. At the end of each day, Randy's son Todd and

I stayed late and each hit a bucket of balls. We would then pick up the balls in the outfield and go back and do it again.

During the summer of 1985, Randy called and asked if I would come to a Cubs mini camp in Chicago again. He told me he would waive the fees if I would go back to Arizona the next winter. We were in Wrigley Field for the big game at Cubs mini camp. Bob Gibson, a retired baseball pitcher who played 17 seasons for the Cardinals, was in town and suited up with the pros. In practice, I had hit a ball off the 368-foot marker in left center field, as well as fouling a few balls over the fence. I was one of the last batters of the day when it came to my second at bat.

The Cubs were playing right after us, so there were about 10,000 fans in Wrigley Field. I was at the plate, and Bob was pitching. I fouled the first pitch down the left field line, and I swung and foul tipped the second pitch. The third pitch was a change up, and I could have swung about three times before the ball made it to Randy's catcher's mitt. I had never heard so many boo's in my life—they were booing at me.

"I know how you hit the ball," Bob said when he came up to me after the game. "I just couldn't resist the changeup."

He shook my hand, and we all went to the locker room.

On January 16, 1986, our son Matthew Jay Kirkpatrick was born prematurely. He died soon after being born. It is difficult when life is taken away. God helped my wife and me through the situation, and we accept His will. We learned to always be thankful for what God has given us and to allow time to heal our wounds. Susan had such a difficult time with this pregnancy that we thought we should be thankful for the three girls we had. As much as I would like to have had a son, I know sons-in-law will be great.

I attended Randy Hundley's baseball camp again in 1986, and this time we left Jenna with family. On this trip, Susan spent more time at the park with Laura and Andrea. I was having a great time playing baseball while they were at the park and doing homework. Todd Hundley and I were always the last to leave the ball park with our two buckets of balls and pitching machine. Once again, Randy called and proposed that if I came to his camp in Chicago, he would waive the fee if I attended camp in Arizona in the winter. Susan and I talked it over and decided to go back to Chicago. The three-day mini camp was always a thrill because you didn't know which major league players would be there.

That year some of Susan's and my family came to watch the big game between the campers and the 1969 Cubs. I think the real players enjoyed watching us campers. When game time came around, I couldn't find Susan and the girls—or her mother, aunt or sister. I found out later that as they were leaving the restaurant from breakfast, little Andrea had wandered ahead. The next thing they knew, she was getting into one of the elevators at the Westin Hotel, and the door was closing. Andrea spent some time on the elevators—there were three of them—with Susan and her family split up trying to find her. Susan's aunt Bonnie found her on the second floor. She was exiting a different elevator than the first one she had gone into. It was a good thing Susan didn't tell me until after the game.

Later on that year, I was with Andrea at a 40th wedding anniversary at the Wesleyan Church in Greentown. There were three girls sitting on the covered organ bench with their legs tucked under them, and Andrea thought she could join them. Somehow she lost her balance and fell off the bench, breaking her arm in two places. You could see the broken bones through the skin, so I loaded Andrea into the car, and we headed to the ER. I was going about 45 miles per hour in a 30-mile-per-hour zone when—you guessed it—I was stopped by the new town marshal. He asked where I was going in such a hurry, and I told him that my daughter had broken her arm and I was taking her to the hospital. After exchanging a few words, Andrea and I were on our way to the hospital again.

***

During the winter of 1986, we were on our way back to Randy Hundley's baseball camp in Scottsdale, Arizona. The team this year was a little different from the year before. We had this old guy that owned a famous, very expensive clothing store in Chicago. He went to right field and stood there every day. He fielded the ball, but he couldn't run, couldn't throw, and was an automatic out at the plate. Some of the guys gave him a hard time, but I never did. We were on our fourth game for the week, and I had made some unbelievable plays in the field. It was my turn at bat, and the first pitch came in. I hit it out of the park, across a four-lane highway into grass next to a motel pool. One of my teammates got the ball for me. I still have it today.

Todd and I stayed and hit more balls after everyone went in to shower. The next morning I came in to get dressed, and Al Hrabosky met me at the door. He told me that there had never been a camper to hit a ball out of the park in Randy Hundley's baseball camps in the big game. I kind of ignored him and went to the locker. Al Hrabosky then came over to me with a wooden bat and broke it over the bench I was sitting on. He called me a bad name and said, "You will not hit another ball out of the park. You are a farmer. You're not a pro." Everyone knew I was a farmer. Ever since the 1984 camp, I'd had the nickname of "Country" that Randy Hundley gave me.

The old man that owned the clothing store was getting dressed next to me and said, "You may be able to hit the ball out of the park, but you couldn't afford a tie in my store."

"You're probably right," I said.

Saturday was the big game—the campers against the pros. The first time I batted, Fergie Jenkins came to the plate and told me he was going to put the ball down the middle and that he wanted me to hit the ball out of the park. He did put the ball right down the middle, and I hit the ball well, but not quite hard enough to get over the fence. Fergie was still pitching, but about three batters before I was at bat again, Al Hrabosky came in out of the outfield and told Randy Hundley that he was going to pitch. Al threw some warm-up pitches, and the first fellow that faced him didn't have a chance—Al threw 90-mile-per-hour fast balls. Randy tried to get him to simmer down, but Al told Randy he was preparing for Country. The next batter was a sports writer from Chicago, and he was a pretty good player. Al fired fast balls to him, and he kept fouling them off. He finally flied out. I was up next, and Al came to the plate and told me he was going to strike me out. I decided to choke up on the bat about 2-1/2 to 3 inches so I would have better control. The first pitch came at my head.

"You feel like you're in the pros now?" Al taunted.

Randy told Al to throw strikes, and the next pitch came at my ankles. I just barely got out of the way. Randy called time and asked me if I wanted Fergie to come back up and pitch. I said I would but that Al had started a war, and I would beat his challenge. What I didn't know was that Susan was very upset, and the girls were crying. I told Randy that Al could pitch, but throwing at my head and my body was not acceptable. The next pitch came in high. It hit the lens on the TV recording camera. The next pitch came in, and I fouled into the backstop. The next pitch was high and outside. I decided to choke up another half inch on the bat because Al was throwing smoke. It was like that ball was coming out of a cannon. The next pitch came in, and I hit it directly to the right fielder who was playing within 50 feet of the right field fence. I had won the battle. He didn't strike me out. He came at me and started yelling. I thought he was putting on a show for the 3,000 or 4,000 fans that were in the bleachers, so I ignored him. However, he wasn't putting on a show, and Randy came out and got him.

"You will never hit another ball out of the park as long as I am pitching!" Al screamed. He didn't even talk to me at the banquet.

A few months later Randy called me and asked me to come to the Cardinals camp in St. Louis at no charge. He said that after what happened to me in Arizona, he owed me that much. So, we loaded the family up and went to St. Louis, so Dad could play in the Cardinals stadium. Red Schoendienst and Joe Cunningham were both there—along with Al Hrabosky. We had three practice days in Cardinals stadium with some rain delays. I was again hitting the ball well. I played third base, and Al Hrabosky came to me and apologized for his actions in Arizona. He said I could have been hurt really badly, but he knew I was a good athlete and could take it. He said he just couldn't get over a farmer hitting the ball out of the park like a pro. For the Friday night Cardinals game, he gave me nine tickets on the front row between home plate and the Cardinals dug out.

It was Saturday, and we were ready for the big game—the campers against the pros. My first time up, Al Hrabosky was pitching, and Randy Hundley was catching. Al came marching to the plate like a mad bull. I was worried. He told me he was going to get Jenna and bring her down to the field. He climbed over the side wall, walked up the steps, picked up Jenna and brought her to home plate. Al proceeded to tell Jenna that her dad was a good ball player. Then, out of the blue, he said he was going to pick her dad apart and barbecue him. Jenna started crying, and we took her to the wall to Susan. Al then returned to the plate and told me that he really had meant his apology. He was going to pitch the balls down the middle, so I could hit one out of the park. I hit the first pitch over the fence about three feet over the foul line. The second pitch I fouled again. The third pitch was down the middle. I swung and missed.

CHAPTER 12

Running the Fair

1988-1990

THE BECK'S DEALER TRIP in 1988 was to the Grand Cayman Islands, and I arranged for Mom and Dad to go on the trip as well. Their 40th wedding anniversary was February 25, 1988. We had a great time that week with them and many other friends. Lee Rulon and Sonny Beck planned an anniversary party on an old-time sail boat. It was a surprise to my parents, and Lee set up everything. About three-quarters of the group went on the huge sailboat. Lee had food catered and brought on a case of wine.

1988 was a drought year but not quite as bad as 1983. It was a learning year for me because I found out what two or three-tenths of an inch of rain can do for soybeans the first week in August. The railroad track north of us about three miles was the dividing line of those two- or three-tenths of an inch of rain. We got two or three-tenths off and on from the middle of July to the middle of August. Those little rains made 15 bushels difference per acre in soybean yields south of the railroad tracks. Our corn was about 140 bushels per acre, and our beans were 57. North of the tracks the corn was around 130 bushels to the acre, and beans were about 42. This proves every little bit of rain helps in a dry year.

This was also my first year as co-chairman of the Howard County 4-H Fair. I had been chairman of the clean-up committee for the previous several years and spent a lot of time at the chiropractor's office due to lifting and dumping so many barrels of trash—starting at 4:30 every morning. I was very glad to be offered the position of co-chairman, if for no other reason than to get off the clean-up committee. I asked Dick Keyton, fair chairman, if he had a job description for me. He told me I would learn as I went, and that's the way it was for the next two years. I soon learned that the fair chairman and co-chairman were kind of honorary positions. Each chairman was organized, and the committee members knew what their roles were. This is why the Howard County 4-H Fair is one of the most successful county fairs in the state of Indiana.

I helped Jay take money from vendors, and it didn't take me long to tell him that his bookkeeping and billing were out of date. He let me develop a computer program in DataStar and ReportStar in which we could do the billing, record payments, have a comment line for each vendor, and have all the bills for the next year ready to print by making one keystroke. What I didn't tell him that day was that I already had the program made for my farm business and seed business. In those years of my life I worked all day. When farm records needed to be entered, I did that after I got home. A lot of times I didn't get to bed before 2:00 a.m. I had developed my own accounting system and tracked expenses and income for every field that we farmed. Jay asked me if I would help him in the office, and when my term was up as fair chairman in 1991, I became his co-secretary.

In 1989, Jay received an application from a food vendor who wanted to come to our fair. The name of the vendor was Gabby Food Concessions. He sent great pictures of his display, had a food menu of steak, chicken, and so on—all of which looked good from the pictures. Gabby also sent a professional drawing of the layout he wanted. Jay told Gabby that we did not have room for the layout he wanted and what we could do for him space-wise. Gabby came to the fair for setup, and of course he didn't have the space he wanted, so he went to my father, Robert Kirkpatrick.

Dad was either chairman or co-chairman of the tent and space committee at the time.

Jay was away from the fair on insurance business, and Dad came to me and told me we didn't leave enough space for Gabby. I told Dad I had the report laid out correctly and filled him in on what Gabby wanted and what we could provide. Dad went down and told Gabby, who became crazy mad, so Dad brought him to the office where we had a verbal knock-down drag-out. Gabby called me every name in the book. He described how great of a display he had, explained that he had sent his money in and expected all the space he had asked for. I told him that I was with Jay when he told him what space we had available and if additional space opened, then he could have it. The additional space had not opened up, and he immediately demanded his money back. I refused to return his down payment until Monday evening, and he threatened to sue me and the fair.

"Gabby," I said, "maybe we should kick you off the fair grounds now."

He told me he wasn't leaving until he got his refund. I told him that if he didn't change his attitude I could call the sheriff's department and have him removed from the fair. He stormed out of the office and did not continue to set up that day. I told Jay what had happened, so in the event that Gabby showed up, he would know what was going on. Gabby approached Jay later in the day, and Jay told him he would have to deal with me. Jay is usually the "good guy" at the fair, and I handle most of the disputes. That's the way our personalities work.

The next afternoon I was in our electrical building. I came out and headed back toward the office when I saw Gabby coming at me like a mad bull. He had a three-foot tent stake with him. I thought he was coming to attack me, and I looked for a board or anything to defend myself with, but nothing was close. I did see Dad across the fair, but I couldn't get his attention. I didn't want to have a physical fight with Gabby, but it looked like it was inevitable. Gabby was within ten feet of me, and I was nervous.

He then came closer and said, "I owe you an apology." I breathed a sigh of relief. Gabby asked me what was wrong. I told him I thought he was coming to beat me with the tent stake.

"No," he said. "I saw you, and I was coming to apologize to you for my actions and wanted to ask if we could forget what happened."

I told him I would never forget what happened, but if he wanted to comply with our rules and set up in the space we had available, it was OK. From that time on, Gabby treated Jay, my father and me with the utmost respect. After 1989, Gabby got the space he wanted, and in years to come much more. As of 2015, Gabby is still at the Howard County 4-H Fair.

1990 was my first year as chairman of the Howard County 4-H Fair. Jay and I had always discussed the open space in front of the fair office which is west all the way to the livestock barn. I told Jay we needed to continue the road from Payton Street North to the midway. Then we would have another road to sell vendor frontage. We were finally able to agree on the road. It was unofficially named Bryan Kirkpatrick Boulevard.

Arden D. was the publisher of the *Kokomo Tribune.* I knew him through his wife, and he wanted to give $25,000 to have a famous person perform at our fair. We were able to book Louise Mandrell, and it was known as the *Kokomo Tribune* Louise Mandrell Show. It was a great show. In 1991, we booked Lori Morgan, and our fair was very appreciative of Arden and the *Kokomo Tribune* for their sponsorships.

I had four great years as co-chairman and chairman of the Howard County 4-H Fair. Our girls also participated in many 4-H activities at the fair. The Pioneer Village had a tradition of parades with teams of ponies and antique tractors. Ponies harnessed to a buckboard were used in almost every parade, but in the last parade of the year, something spooked the ponies, and we had a runaway team of ponies and buckboard just like in the movies. The horses bolted from the north end of the fairground to the south end at full speed. The queen and her court were on the buckboard, along with the driver. The driver and another girl were hurt pretty badly, and people walking into the fair got hit by the horses. After all the great times we had at the fair during the entire week, this had to happen. The memories of all the good things that had happened were now overshadowed by this terrible accident. The news stations from Indianapolis came and interviewed people. I reluctantly agreed to the interviews. The driver and the girl healed, but my thoughts and prayers are still with them.

***

We had a great team of school board members in 1990. I am not sure the public realized what we accomplished in those years. In 1988, we came up with the idea of filming the teachers in their classrooms and then reviewing what they had taught. Dr. Hill wrote and applied for a grant for the project. We had to make sure that Project Teacher, as it was called, would never be used as an evaluation tool, because the teacher's association would not agree to it. Instead, we proposed that the teachers that taught the same classes review their work together or review each other's styles and methods of teaching. We received the grant for Project Teacher in 1989. It included some of the teachers going to other schools and explaining the program.

Project Teacher eventually became a hit on the national level, and our school received a letter from the United States Secretary of Education requesting it present Project Teacher at the National School Board Association Convention in New Orleans in the spring of 1990. Dr. Hill was superintendent, and the board members besides me were Bill Begeman, Dennis Maple, Ron Musgrave, Jef Buckley and our school corporation treasurer Verna Rush. As a group, we decided we would take our families to New Orleans when we made the presentation. I want to make it clear that we each paid for our families. We got to New Orleans, and the kids and mothers had a blast at the pool while the rest of us were at the convention center preparing to talk about Project Teacher and attending other presentations. Our group not only went to school board meetings for routine business but also tried to look at every area of education in our school to see what we could do better. We had started a program for the community's input a few years earlier and learned a lot from it. We did our best to implement their top ten concerns.

CHAPTER 13

An Expanding World

1992-1997

BOB McCORMACK, OUR HOWARD COUNTY Extension agent, had been talking to me for some time about the Indiana Agricultural Leadership Program. Time was getting near to have my application in, but I told Bob I didn't feel like I could be away from the farm one weekend every other month, especially in planting and harvest. If there was a commitment made to attend, you were expected to be there. I told Bob I appreciated him talking to me, but I wanted to see the goals and the objectives of this two-year commitment. Bob insisted I would learn leadership skills that would open my mind to the rest of the world, from social interactions to world economic and cultural issues. He promised, if I were to be selected, that I wouldn't be disappointed. I talked to Susan that evening and decided to turn in the application. I was selected for Class V of the Indiana Agricultural Institute. What we didn't know when I applied was that Susan's cousin, Scott Maple, was selected as well.

The first meeting of the IALP in 1992 was in January. It is a two-year course that meets approximately six times a year. In the first meeting we had a Myers Briggs personality test. I had no idea what I was getting into. We took the test, and I learned that people have different types of personalities. I learned about introverts and extroverts, and I discovered that I am an extrovert. I learned that some people are sensitive or intuitive, and I discovered I was a very sensitive person. The next category was thinking or feeling. I learned some people are thinkers—they look for a logical explanation or solution for everything. Others have feelings and are concerned with harmony. The test showed that I was a thinker. The last category was judging versus perception. This test showed that I fit into the perception category by a large margin, making me an ESTP—one of 16 types of personalities.

This test may be one of the most important studies I have ever done, as it helped me understand people who are introverts. Previously, I thought some people didn't like me because I was always the one to start a conversation with them. As a result of the class, I started viewing these people differently, and I am sure it has made me a better person. As an extrovert, it was hard for me to understand an introvert. I very quickly learned that God put each of us on this earth with different personalities, all of which are good. However, we are made differently and need to learn to adapt before judging another person who doesn't have the same personality we do.

For the next meeting, we spent a week in Washington, D.C., and discovered firsthand how our government operates, learning history that wasn't taught in our schools. The next several meetings we traveled to different parts of the state of Indiana listening to speakers who were expert leaders in the agricultural industry. We visited ports in northern and southern Indiana and saw coal mines and how land was reclaimed for agricultural use. While we were in Terra Haute, we also visited the Indiana Air National Guard Base, touring the shop where they maintained the F16 and F14 fighter jets. I was able to talk to a pilot while there. He asked me where I was from, and I told him Greentown, Indiana. He stated he knew exactly where it was. He then proceeded to describe the grain bins, two grain legs, a tan brick home and a tan tool shed. The pilot noted that they used our grain legs to simulate target practice.

The academic lessons in the twelve sessions have helped me to understand the real world and not just our home community. Before I entered the IALP, I was very closed minded about the world outside of Greentown, Indiana. I learned that, in order to make good decisions, my thoughts had to revolve around not only our own rural communities in public affairs, but they should also include those at the state, national and international levels.

Our overseas educational trip was to France. Our base was in Chartres, and we were all introduced to Jossette, a college professor there. We were made to feel welcome, but I had a problem with the language and couldn't pick up on it as quickly as some. We toured churches, castles and much more. We had lunch and dinner with French leaders and got their perspectives on agriculture as well. We were taken to ports where they import and export grain, and I learned very quickly that I had to eat the bread because they all insisted on us drinking wine, and sometimes whiskey. I was told by one of the French families I stayed with that, if I was not used to drinking, I must eat a lot of bread to prevent a hangover. In other words, drink the wine and whiskey and eat the bread—or insult the French people. We had a great time. In some places I was described as the "big American farmer."

The first family I stayed with lived about 100 miles southwest of Chartres. Their son, Sylvan, was a student at the agricultural college where our home base was. One night, Sylvan's mother prepared a seven-course meal for us. I was car sick from the ride to the farm, and when we went into the living room, Sylvan's father tried to get me to have a drink before our meal. Since we couldn't communicate well, I finally accepted some kind of whiskey. It tasted terrible, and I wanted to eat bread to see if I could get to feeling better. Sylvan's mother finally said dinner was served. We had seven different kinds of cheese, and Sylvan's mother wanted to know which one I liked best. I pointed to two or three of the cheeses. I learned very quickly that was not acceptable. Sylvan's brother informed me that I should have chosen one, not three. I had insulted his mother.

I asked him to explain to her that was not my intent. I finally picked the goat cheese, and they laughed hard for about five minutes. I'm still not sure what was so funny to them. Our main course was cow stomach, and when I asked for more bread, they refilled my wine glass. All I could think of was that it seemed like I drank more booze in that one night than I had in my whole life. The bread was helping, but my nose was numb. We finally finished our meal, and they took me upstairs to my room. I was so sick, but there was a bathroom in my room, and I prayed that I wouldn't heave. I got to sleep, and they woke me up at daylight. I was feeling really rough, but I managed to go downstairs for breakfast. I did not want to eat, but I choked down enough to keep Sylvan's mother from being disappointed in me—I already had one strike against me.

The family managed to tell me that we were going to Sylvan's grandparents' and uncle's farm. I hoped I would start feeling better, and I did turn a corner around 11 a.m. when we pulled into the farm. The family was so excited to see an American, the first thing we had to do was go into the kitchen and have some whiskey. I first declined, but I could tell very quickly that was not going to be accepted. I asked for bread to go with my whiskey, and they laughed and laughed while getting me the bread.

I learned from Sylvan's mother that there had been battles between the Germans and the Americans behind their house. Sylvan's grandfather told me that they still find mortar shells that didn't detonate. American soldiers saved many of their friends' lives during the war by providing medicine and chocolate. After about two drinks and six slices of homemade bread, they took me outside and showed me where battles had taken place. We then visited their swine facilities.

We left the farm and went to a golf course where pro golfers had played. While we were there, I met a female worker who spoke good English. For the first time since being at Sylvan's home, I felt like I was alive again and not just having a dream that I was not able to communicate well. The girl answered a lot of questions for me and explained many confusing cultural issues. I asked her to explain to Sylvan's mother that I didn't intend to disappoint her when I picked three different kinds of cheese as my favorite instead of one. The girl told me French culture is very precise in answering questions like that, and I had dodged the question. When she apologized to Sylvan's mother for me, everyone laughed and said something about the big American farmer. I still don't know what they said, but it sure gave them a laugh.

Back at Sylvan's farm, we went inside to have whiskey again before dinner. I asked for bread right away. We then had another seven-course meal. I'm not sure what it was, but it was very good. The next morning we headed out for the town of Le Mans where the famous race is. While driving into town, I saw some buildings that were in bad shape. I asked why they didn't tear the buildings down and build new ones. Sylvan's brother translated.

"No, no, no, no," his mother said emphatically. "We restore buildings not tear them down."

Our group traveled on a high-speed train from Paris to Lyon and had lunch up on a hill inside of a cave. Wine was a must for everyone, but I held off until I got some bread. Most of us who ate the bread were in good shape. While back at Chartres, we also toured the Normandy Beaches, a sacred site. As we walked in the sand at Omaha Beach, I couldn't believe that our officers had our soldiers fighting a physical uphill battle there. When seeing the contour of the land, you would not think the American soldiers had a chance. It was moving to visit the Normandy American Cemetery and Memorial and see how many crosses were in that cemetery. This cemetery was the cleanest and best-kept area that I saw in the entire country of France.

The last night before heading back to the USA a large party was thrown for the Americans by the college and the parents of the students at the college. It should have taken us approximately 40 minutes to get to the place to eat, but we had to wait on the road. French farmers were protesting against the Americans. There was a long negotiation, and finally we were let through. The leader of the protesters joined us for dinner, but he was not a happy person.

We had a whole hog roasted on a rod for dinner. In France, families don't sit together when at parties. They sit with neighbors and friends so they can visit. I was sitting with Mrs. Hulet and some of her friends. They had something they wanted me to try, and they were all giggling at the same time. I was instructed to take a small cube of sugar and dip it in a glass. Come to find out, it was cognac. I started in on the bread because these ladies would not take "No" for an answer when it came to dipping more sugar cubes in cognac.

Later on in the evening, I met with the leader of the protesting farmers. There was an interpreter right there with us, and I held my hand out to shake hands with him. He would not shake my hand, and the interpreter said something to him. I said I wanted to give him my Indiana Agricultural lapel pin, and I told him to not hold the American farmer accountable for our government leaders' policies.

"We are just like you," I said, "and would rather not have so much government interference."

I asked him to believe in the American farmer as he would the French farmer who just wants what is fair, and I told him we should take the strengths of each country and build on them. I explained there was no reason farmers of both countries couldn't work together. As time went on, the gentleman softened. The translator repeated all of what I said to him. I again offered my Indiana Agricultural pin to him, and the translator told me to pin it on his collar. I did so, and the French farmer then shook my hand. I never saw him again.

While in France we had an evening dinner cruise on the Seine River, spent a lot of time in the Louvre museum, went to the top of the Eiffel Tower and walked around the Arc de Triomphe. One of the first nights in France we ate at a steakhouse and some of the guys suggested I order steak tartar. They told me that was the best item on the menu. While we were waiting for our food, I was amazed at all the dogs in this very fancy restaurant. My steak came, and it was raw. The waiter and everyone at the table busted out laughing. I was stunned at first, and then I realized what the guys had done to me. The waiter took the steak to the kitchen and cooked it to medium. It was very good.

The time spent with our French friends was an experience I will never forget. When we got back to Cincinnati, I was glad to see Susan and the girls. They all came at me with big hugs and tears. When we got back home, Class V had several more meetings, and in December, our wives joined us for the Friday evening and Saturday meetings. Bob McCormack was right. The Indiana Agricultural Leadership Program taught me how to be more effective in my speaking and writing skills, to be more thoughtful when analyzing public issues from various perspectives, and to better understand aspects of economics and culture. Sylvan and Fabrice, two friends I met in France, came to my farm the following summer. Sylvan could only stay for a day, but Fabrice was with us for six weeks.

***

In 1993, our school board went back to New Orleans for the National School Boards Association Convention. We had heard some interesting presentations about education that we thought we could possibly take back to implement in our school. Technology, computers and software of all kinds were at this show. When the shows were over, we ate at Felix's—shrimp and gumbo—the entire time we were there. I had an interest in boats and ships—especially those carrying grain, so I spent a lot of time at the waterfront. I had never seen so many air conditioners and John Deere tractors waiting to be loaded on a ship. The other guys went back to the hotel, and I explored a gambling boat. I walked through the boat and saw that it was about time to meet the group for our evening dinner. When I attempted to get off the boat, I discovered that we were not docked. As a result, I was about 45 minutes late for our group dinner because I had to wait for the boat to return to the dock before I could get off.

We had dinner with the folks from the Skillman Company. It was Harold Skillman's birthday, and one of his employees and I arranged for a person dressed up as a gorilla to pick on Harold during dinner. The restaurant manager came to our table and told me I had a phone call. It was the booking company for the gorilla. The gorilla act wasn't going to be available, and they asked if they could send another act. I said sure. As we finished our meal and the waiters were serving dessert, this nice-looking lady came in with a mink coat. There were about 60 of the Skillman Company's guests in the room and a girl about 15 years old. This lady performed well—except a little too much. We all survived the evening, and of course I got the blame for the show. Harold's employee begged me to not tell Harold that he and I hired the gorilla together, let alone the stripper. I told him this was New Orleans. I called the company and asked why they sent a stripper. They said that was all that was available. The stripper never really bared her parts, but she sure did embarrass Harold and made the rest of us very nervous. Harold's wife, Barb, wasn't thrilled either.

We made it home from New Orleans, and Susan took my camera film to get the pictures developed. A few days later, Susan picked up the pictures. When I came in from work that day, I could tell something was wrong with Susan. The kids went to bed, and she showed me some really nasty pictures. I told her I had no idea how they got on my camera. That wasn't a good enough explanation. I finally remembered that I had given Ron and Jef my bag, which had my camera in it, the evening I toured the gambling boat. I told her that they must have taken those photos on the way back to the hotel. At the next board meeting, I confronted Ron and Jef, and of course they denied it. Before we went home that evening, Verna told me what they had done. I explained to Susan later that night that what I had told her was indeed what happened. I told her that Verna said if she had any more questions to call her. Well, that is all it took for Susan to know that I was set up.

It was 1994 or 1995 when Beck's sponsored a dealer trip to the Cayman Islands. This time, Lee Rulon wanted to go diving with me and several other close friends. I took the test in the swimming pool and passed, so Butch, the instructor, took about five of us out in the water. We had to pass another test, which was to go down to the ocean floor and sit in a circle. Each of us had to take our mask off, put it back on and then clear it. We went down a rope tied to the boat, and when I started down, my head felt like it was going to explode. Working my way up and down, I did everything Butch told me to get my head to clear. All of a sudden it cleared. I slowly went to the bottom and sat with the rest of the crew. We removed our masks one by one and then put them on and cleared them. I'm just glad I was breathing through my mouth. After we finished our test, the instructor let us swim around for a while and look at rocks and fish. Butch came and directed me to work my way up to the surface. I was getting low on oxygen in my tank. I slowly made it to the top and was feeling pretty good—except for my head.

That evening Lee had it set up for Butch to take us out for a night dive. There were about eight of us, and everyone was in the water but Butch and me. A boat came by with people on it shooting a gun. I told Butch that I would stay on the surface and protect the boat, but he pushed me in instead. I didn't really have enough weight on my waist, but I managed to get down with the others. We each had a flashlight, and Lee and I followed Butch. We went in between some big rocks, and Butch set off fire works on the ocean floor. When everyone left, I guess I went the wrong way and couldn't find them. I was nervous because I didn't have enough weight on and was coming to the top too fast. There was nothing I could do to stop it, and Butch and Lee found me and got me to the boat.

We got in that night and my whole body felt like I had air bubbles in my blood. I had a terrible time the next day, and I went to the dive shop and told the fellow what happened. He explained I came up too quickly and was experiencing the bends. He told me that I needed to dive again but go down real slow and come up real slow. This might cure the bends. I told Lee what had happened, so he set up a dive the next day to go through a sunken ship. Lee told Butch about my case of the bends. When I got ready to go down, Butch said he was going with me all the way down. I was not to move until he signaled. When we got to the bottom, the pain was gone. Lee kept checking my oxygen levels because I was breathing really hard. Then Butch told me it was time to go up. He stayed with me all the way, and when I got to the top, all of my pain was gone. That was my third and final dive.

***

In early 1994, we decided to remodel our home on 1100 East. We took out a bedroom on the east side of the kitchen and made it all one room. We also took out another room on the east side of the living room and made that one big room. We had to move the stairway, and that ended up being a mess. The girls, Susan and I still wonder today how we were all able to get to the right places at the right time. When you have a child getting ready to graduate from high school, it provides a good excuse to remodel the house—especially if you have open house at your home after graduation.

Laura graduated from high school in 1995. Since I was on the school board, I was able to hand Laura her diploma. She was a good student in school, and she always wanted to do what was right. I had to be careful how I chose my words in some situations because it didn't take much to make Laura cry. She ran cross country, played basketball until her senior year and was a varsity starter on the softball team starting her freshman year. Laura played on some very good teams that came close to winning the state championship on at least two occasions. Unless we were planting, Dad and I quit working to go watch the games.

Andrea started on the varsity softball team as a freshman as well. She had always batted right-handed, and she was so fast in running and movement that Jerry had her try batting left-handed and perfecting the drag bunt. When I coached Andrea in Pixie league I never thought about having her bat left because she hit so well right-handed. She had a lot of power for a smaller girl. As it turned out, after four years of softball batting left-handed, Andrea held the school records for batting average, on base percentage, stolen bases and then some.

CHAPTER 14

An Emptying Nest

1997

IT WAS THE FALL OF 1997, and Susan, Andrea, Jenna and I went to the University of Evansville to meet Laura, who was a junior there. It was a Saturday morning, and we were gathered for breakfast at Bob Evans. Conversation was good, and we were especially glad to see Laura, who was extremely happy to see us. However, I could tell something was wrong. It wasn't long before Laura burst into tears. I finally got her calmed down and asked her what was wrong. Laura proceeded to tell me that she wasn't sure where she was going to fit in life.

"Who will my friends be when I get out of college?" she asked. "Will I be able to get a job, will I ever get married, where will I live?"

The questions continued.

"Put your trust in God," I said. "Ask Him to be with you, ask Him to guide you, ask Him to give you wisdom. Most of all, when an opportunity is put before you, take time to ask Him if that is His will for you."

I continued, telling her that she should put her faith in God and trust Him, seeking to be patient and staying in tune with Him every day.

"God works through people," I explained, "so be sure to listen to the people you know trust in God."

I told her about *The Power of Positive Thinking,* a book by Norman Vincent Peale that helped change my life. It taught me that nothing can become a thing until it is once a thought. Not all thoughts become things, but God directs you to those thoughts that need to become things. Because of the message of that book and the words of my father I decided I could do anything that anyone else could do. I knew I might not be able to do it as fast or as good, but I could do it—and I *would* do it. It wasn't long before Laura's opportunity arose. She decided to become a minister and applied to Garrett Theological Seminary. Sometimes one has to hit bottom before God can do His work. The closer you are to God, the easier these problems will be to solve. You have a choice to go with God or go it alone and make your life miserable.

I learned this while I was on the school board in 1980. When challenges came up, I would sometimes forget to ask God for help in that moment. Many times I would drive to a school board meeting and ask God to change the hearts of two board members that I clashed with. Every time I asked God to guide me, He provided the help I needed. I pushed so hard for education first and sports second that it sometimes became a knock-down drag-out fight in the meetings. The superintendent had been there since I was in the first grade, and he took me aside—as a father, not as a boss.

"I have seen you come up through the grades, watched you play baseball, football and basketball," Mr. Dewitt told me. "I really respect you because when you did something on the field, you gave it all you had."

He noted, however, that, if I had worked as hard in the classroom as I had on the ball field, I would have been a straight-A student. This discussion took place in the winter of 1981, and it cemented

d, telling her that she should put her faith in God and
eeking to be patient and staying in tune with Him

s through people," I explained, "so be sure to listen to
u know trust in God."

about *The Power of Positive Thinking*, a book by
ent Peale that helped change my life. It taught me
an become a thing until it is once a thought. Not all
me things, but God directs you to those thoughts
ecome things. Because of the message of that book
s of my father I decided I could do anything that
uld do. I knew I might not be able to do it as fast or
ould do it—and I *would* do it. It wasn't long before
unity arose. She decided to become a minister and
rett Theological Seminary. Sometimes one has to
ore God can do His work. The closer you are to
these problems will be to solve. You have a choice
or go it alone and make your life miserable.

while I was on the school board in 1980. When
e up, I would sometimes forget to ask God for
ment. Many times I would drive to a school board
God to change the hearts of two board members
ith. Every time I asked God to guide me, He
lp I needed. I pushed so hard for education first
d that it sometimes became a knock-down drag-
meetings. The superintendent had been there
e first grade, and he took me aside—as a father,

u come up through the grades, watched you play
and basketball," Mr. Dewitt told me. "I really
use when you did something on the field, you
."

ver, that, if I had worked as hard in the classroom
ll field, I would have been a straight-A student.
ok place in the winter of 1981, and it cemented

---

to the ocean floor and sit in a circle. Each of us had to take our mask off, put it back on and then clear it. We went down a rope tied to the boat, and when I started down, my head felt like it was going to explode. Working my way up and down, I did everything Butch told me to get my head to clear. All of a sudden it cleared. I slowly went to the bottom and sat with the rest of the crew. We removed our masks one by one and then put them on and cleared them. I'm just glad I was breathing through my mouth. After we finished our test, the instructor let us swim around for a while and look at rocks and fish. Butch came and directed me to work my way up to the surface. I was getting low on oxygen in my tank. I slowly made it to the top and was feeling pretty good—except for my head.

That evening Lee had it set up for Butch to take us out for a night dive. There were about eight of us, and everyone was in the water but Butch and me. A boat came by with people on it shooting a gun. I told Butch that I would stay on the surface and protect the boat, but he pushed me in instead. I didn't really have enough weight on my waist, but I managed to get down with the others. We each had a flashlight, and Lee and I followed Butch. We went in between some big rocks, and Butch set off fire works on the ocean floor. When everyone left, I guess I went the wrong way and couldn't find them. I was nervous because I didn't have enough weight on and was coming to the top too fast. There was nothing I could do to stop it, and Butch and Lee found me and got me to the boat.

We got in that night and my whole body felt like I had air bubbles in my blood. I had a terrible time the next day, and I went to the dive shop and told the fellow what happened. He explained I came up too quickly and was experiencing the bends. He told me that I needed to dive again but go down real slow and come up real slow. This might cure the bends. I told Lee what had happened, so he set up a dive the next day to go through a sunken ship. Lee told Butch about my case of the bends. When I got ready to go down, Butch said he was going with me all the way down. I was not to move until he signaled. When we got to the bottom, the pain was gone. Lee kept checking my oxygen levels because I was breathing really hard. Then Butch told me it was time to go up. He stayed with me all the way, and when I got to the top, all of my pain was gone. That was my third and final dive.

***

In early 1994, we decided to remodel our home on 1100 East. We took out a bedroom on the east side of the kitchen and made it all one room. We also took out another room on the east side of the living room and made that one big room. We had to move the stairway, and that ended up being a mess. The girls, Susan and I still wonder today how we were all able to get to the right places at the right time. When you have a child getting ready to graduate from high school, it provides a good excuse to remodel the house—especially if you have open house at your home after graduation.

Laura graduated from high school in 1995. Since I was on the school board, I was able to hand Laura her diploma. She was a good student in school, and she always wanted to do what was right. I had to be careful how I chose my words in some situations because it didn't take much to make Laura cry. She ran cross country, played basketball until her senior year and was a varsity starter on the softball team starting her freshman year. Laura played on some very good teams that came close to winning the state championship on at least two occasions. Unless we were planting, Dad and I quit working to go watch the games.

Andrea started on the varsity softball team as a freshman as well. She had always batted right-handed, and she was so fast in running and movement that Jerry had her try batting left-handed and perfecting the drag bunt. When I coached Andrea in Pixie league I never thought about having her bat left because she hit so well right-handed. She had a lot of power for a smaller girl. As it turned out, after four years of softball batting left-handed, Andrea held the school records for batting average, on base percentage, stolen bases and then some.

CHA

An Emp

1997

IT WAS THE FALL OF
I went to the University
a junior there. It was a Sat
for breakfast at Bob Evans,
especially glad to see Laur
However, I could tell som
Laura burst into tears. I f
her what was wrong. Lau
sure where she was going

"Who will my friends
"Will I be able to get a
live?"

The questions continu

"Put your trust in G
Him to guide you, ask
an opportunity is put
His will for you."

I continue
trust Him,
every day.

"God work
the people y

I told her
Norman Vin
that nothing
thoughts bec
that need to b
and the word
anyone else c
as good, but I
Laura's opport
applied to Ga
hit bottom be
God, the easie
to go with God

I learned thi
challenges cam
help in that mo
meeting and as
that I clashed
provided the he
and sports secor
out fight in the
since I was in th
not as a boss.

"I have seen yo
baseball, footbal
respect you beca
gave it all you ha

He noted, howe
as I had on the ba
This discussion to

our commitment to make the kids' education a priority—and sometimes it was he and I against the rest of the board when it came to those issues.

***

On June 11, 1998, our church was making pies to sell at the Greentown Glass Festival. While Susan and Kathy were making pies with several other women of our church, Rex and I went to Kokomo to get something to eat. We were at Rex's when Larry Keiffer called me and asked if we knew about the tornado coming our way. When Rex and I walked around the north side of his house, Rex said he had never seen a tornado before.

"Look over at Deere Knoll," I told him. "You see that house going up into the sky? That is a tornado. We need to get to the basement!"

Rex said he didn't have a basement, so we went into the bathroom and took Ryan and Kristen in with us. By the time we got into the bathroom, the tornado had hit the house. I prayed to God the entire time, and when the tornado had passed, I looked at Rex, Ryan and Kristen. They all looked like Casper the ghost. We were all OK, but we were covered with white dust from insulation in the attic. The dust was so thick we could hardly see in front of us. Several large stones lay on Kristen's bed where her head would have been. As we went outside, we saw the immense damage the tornado had done. I noticed that my truck tire had a three-inch thorn driven into the sidewall. The rest of the truck was OK, but the house and the neighbors' houses weren't so fortunate. That evening we brought the backhoe into town to help get trees and limbs out of the way. We spent the next few days helping people clean up in Greentown. The same tornado that hit Kokomo hit one of my fields and destroyed the trees on the ditch bank.

***

In July of 1998 our farm was one of five to host the Purdue University Cooperative Extension Service and Indiana Farm Management Association tours. Larry Keiffer from Huntington

County had participated in the tour the year before and asked on behalf of Purdue Extension if we would consider being a host in 1998. Larry told us it was a great opportunity to get the tool sheds cleaned and throw away items that were no longer needed. As soon as we finished planting, that is exactly what we did.

Tom Dickover, Kevin Moss, Dad, Mom, Susan and our girls cleaned the shop up. It was good fellowship working toward a common goal. Susan wasn't very excited about the date they chose, but she worked around it. She was a chaperone and cook at church camp that week, so she drove home from Epworth Forest with Andrea and Jenna for the event. They left to go back to camp as soon as it was over.

My father and I participated in the 1998 Farm Progress Show in Windfall, Indiana, with Beck's Hybrids and American Cyanamid. The photo above includes the President of Beck's Superior Hybrids, Sonny Beck; myself; Research Director Kyle Smith; and Vice President of Beck's Superior Hybrids, Scott Beck.

***

It was 1999, and Jenna had played softball every spring until her freshman year in high school. She had a cannon for an arm, was a great shortstop and hit with power. Jenna knew how much her dad loved baseball and didn't want to hurt my feelings by running track instead of playing softball. However, Jenna had run track in junior high and realized that it was her passion. She ended up breaking the school record in the 400-meter dash. If, like Jenna, you have a passion in life, do your best to pursue that passion.

Andrea graduated from high school in 1999. She had been offered college scholarships to play softball but decided she wanted to go to school to study and not have the pressure of playing softball while in college. I wasn't surprised at all. Andrea is the type who lets issues build in her mind and then one day she just lets it out—usually with tears. This was the case when making the decision not to play college softball. She was afraid to talk to me about it because she didn't want to hurt my feelings.

Like Andrea, every person has a different personality. As children grow to be young adults they learn to make decisions. Parents must respect the feelings of their children along the way. It is important to be able to have open communication and to be receptive to each other's opinions. In Andrea's case, we respected her choice not to play college softball, and we were thankful that she chose not to accept the college scholarships.

Laura graduated from the University of Evansville in 1999. When she finally allowed God to direct her into seminary, she looked at many schools. I firmly believe that she was called by God to Garrett Evangelical Seminary. Joe and Julie Breisch helped our family move Laura to her Garrett apartment. On the way to Chicago, the U-Haul truck Joe and I were driving broke down on Indiana State Road 30 near Valparaiso. The power steering belt had broken and caused a few other problems. We were limping down Lake Shore Drive trying to make it to Evanston when I was pulled over. It turns out trucks aren't allowed on Lake Shore Drive. I only had about a mile or so left on that road, but it might as well have been five miles because I still got a ticket and a lecture. We finally made it to Laura's apartment and discovered we had three flights of narrow stairs to take all of her belongings up. That was one tiring day, but it didn't take Laura long to fit right in at Garrett.

While we were visiting Garrett to get Laura registered, someone asked Andrea what she was going to do. Andrea had been planning to attend culinary school in downtown Chicago, but the lady suggested that she look at Kendall College, which was next to Garrett. We made an appointment, and Kendall offered Andrea a nice financial package. The college was very nice, and Andrea and Laura could live together. Needless to say, that made Dad pretty happy. I hadn't been so sure about Andrea living in a dorm downtown or living with Laura and taking the train downtown. Susan had spent all summer taking Andrea to check out culinary schools. The next thing we knew, Kendall College was an option. To make a long story short, Andrea accepted the scholarship to Kendall College, and Laura and Andrea lived together while attending colleges in Evanston, Illinois.

2000

In 2000, Jenna entered the Howard County 4-H Queen contest. Each girl that enters has to have a sponsor, and Jenna's sponsor was Beck's Hybrids and Bryan Kirkpatrick, dealer. Jenna had always been a very pretty girl with a lot of wit to go with it, and I felt she had a good chance of winning, even though she was one of the youngest girls that had entered. She was smart enough to respond to on-the-spot questions with common-sense answers, so we were not surprised when she won the contest. Even though I am chairman of the Fair Planning Committee and secretary of the Howard County 4-H Fair, no one that I know of said that she won because of her dad. The judges didn't even know me. I was so proud of Jenna, but most of all, when the show finished, the first thing she did was call Laura and Andrea—her sisters—to share in her joy. That was a priceless moment for her mother and me.

I do a lot of advertising at the fair and other events as Beck's Hybrids and Bryan Kirkpatrick, dealer, splitting the costs 50-50 with Beck's. Jenna was the second contestant that we had sponsored in the beauty pageant since 1976. The reason we've always promoted 4-H is because of the values that are taught and the responsibilities that the program gives 4-H members in taking on projects and finishing them. The 4-H motto is "Make your best better," and I've found that this is another great rule to live by. When you continue to work hard at making your best better and at the same time treat others as you want to be treated, you then have the best attitude for life.

2001-2002

Andrea graduated from Kendall College on September 14, 2001. She had put her application in to go to Purdue the previous fall, but Purdue was a little slow in getting back to her. In the meantime, I was hoping that Andrea would end up at Purdue, but once again I think the Lord had a different plan for Andrea. Instead, Roosevelt University offered Andrea a very nice scholarship, and it was hard for Andrea to turn it down.

Andrea, with one of her pastry
creations

Near Lake Shore Drive, the university was very close to Grant Park. Andrea accepted the scholarship at Roosevelt University. While in school, Andrea worked as a pastry cook at Bittersweet Pastry Shop and Mid-America Club, a private club located in the

AON building. Her final summer in Chicago she worked as a hostess at the Chicago Yacht Club. In the process, Andrea learned a lot about very rich people. Some of the people were kind and made her feel really good. There were a few that demanded everything in an instant.

She learned that these very few people can make you feel pretty aggravated. It doesn't matter how good, kind or respectful you are, there are always those people who are going to complain. That seems to be their nature, and there is nothing you can do about it except to pray for them. The Bible talks about praying for your enemies, and I can tell you it is easier to pray for them than it is to hold ill feelings toward them. When you pray for them, God is involved. The person may or may not ever change, but He will help you have the right attitude toward them.

CHAPTER 15

A Scare in Chicago

WHILE LAURA WAS IN SEMINARY she also did mission work at Hemenway United Methodist Church near the campus. Thirty-three members of our church went and worked there for three days. We painted, replaced drywall, did some electrical work, made minor repairs to the steep copper roof and just had a good time being together. Laura set everything up, and I was the person who went to Home Depot to get the supplies we needed. I spent a lot of time going back and forth.

We finished our work, and the church made plans to have a picnic for us on Saturday evening. We had a few lights to return to Home Depot, and I told Susan to go with Rex and Kathy to the picnic and I would be there after I had returned the items. I parked way out in the parking lot, so I didn't have to worry about people hitting my truck. When I came back to my truck, there was a very fancy black car parked close to my driver's side door, making it difficult to get in.

A man then appeared, cussing me out and accusing me of putting a scratch on his car. I had a few words with him and said I was calling the police.

"Never mind," he said. "I already called them."

About five minutes later a nice-looking lady drove up, got out of her car and requested my driver's license and truck registration. She was dressed like a police officer, so I gave her the information. I then asked for a copy of the other man's registration and his driver's license. When she said no, I told her I had the right to see it.

The man then told me that she was not a police officer but that we were going to the police station. He told me, using a lot of choice words that I won't mention here, that if I didn't follow him, his hit men would come to my home and kill me and my family. We left the parking lot with the man's car in front, me in the middle, and the woman's car behind, close to my bumper. As best I could tell, he was headed to the Evanston police station. I tried to call Rex, but he didn't answer, and I began to feel like I was running out of options—not to mention I had $1,000 in my wallet.

The man in front made a turn down an alley. I hesitated to turn, but before I knew it the lady was on my bumper and I had no choice but to follow. We got about half way down the alley, when the man stopped. We sat there for about two minutes when I saw an old station wagon headed toward us from the opposite direction. I asked the driver to stop and told her what was going on.

"Would you please stay here until they decide to move?" I asked.

The driver agreed, and about three minutes later, we pulled out. Once we were out of the alley, I bolted away toward the police station, but the man and woman beat me there. When I got out of the truck, the man came after me acting as though he had a pistol in his pocket. He took me to his car and showed me the scratches.

"I am telling the story inside, and you are going to back me up," he told me. "If you don't, I will kill you here and then look up the rest of your family in Indiana."

I walked into the station, and he told his story to the officer, who asked me if his account was correct. I didn't answer, which irritated the officer. The man signed the statement, but I refused. The man and the woman then walked out of the police station, but

I stayed behind. They saw that I wasn't coming, so they came back inside to get me, grabbing me by my arms—one on each side—and taking me out of the station. We had some words outside, and the man told me to shut up and leave.

"If you don't, I will force you into my car," he said, "and we will take you out and finish you off now."

We both left, and I immediately called Jay Freeman, my insurance agent and very close friend. I told him what had happened. He told me I had been conned and instructed me to stay put and wait for a phone call from Hasting Mutual Insurance.

"Jay, this is Saturday evening," I said.

He told me he had an emergency number to call, and an agent would advise me what to do. Sure enough, about 15 minutes later, the agent called and told me I had been scammed. He wanted to know if I got the people's names and license plate number of the other vehicle, and I told him the car had a scratched cardboard plate that I couldn't read. After I told him everything else that happened, he told me to stay in Chicago and go back to the police station Monday morning.

That wasn't too big of a hardship as Joe and Julie Breisch and Susan and I were going to stay a few more days to play golf. The agent gave me his phone number and told me to call him Monday morning too. I then called Rex again, and this time he answered. Everyone was worried about me, and I briefly told him what had happened and that I would be at the picnic as soon as I could. I was still shaking like a leaf inside.

I then called my friend Danny Huston and told him what had happened. He told me to keep my line open and that he was going to call his friend Jeff, who has a Blackwater training facility where police officers and the Navy SEALs train. When Jeff called me, I told him what had happened. He told me not to worry but to make sure the man and woman were not following me. Jeff then asked for the name of the fellow on the police report. I told him the officer wouldn't give me a copy because I wasn't the one filing the report. Jeff also told me to stay in Chicago but to get that report when I went back to the station on Monday morning. If they didn't cooperate, I was to call him.

In the meantime, Rex had called me back and wanted to know if I was OK. I told him I would be as soon as I confirmed that I wasn't being followed. When I made it to the picnic, the party was almost over, and I told Susan, Rex and a few others all the details of my ordeal. I had left the church at 4:00 p.m. I didn't get to the picnic until 8:30.

The following Monday, Joe and I went to the police station and told the officer inside what had happened. The officer still refused to give me the report, so I called the Hastings agent and then Jeff. About 30 minutes later, another officer came out and wanted to know if I was Bryan Kirkpatrick.

"I will give you a copy of the police report," he said, "but it will cost you $10."

I assume it was the Hastings Mutual agent that made that happen, but it could have been Jeff. I called Jeff and explained I had the report. He gave me a number to fax it to and encouraged me not to worry—he had friends in the Chicago police force who would protect me. About three hours later, Jeff called me back to report that his police friends had gone to the address of the con artist. They had informed the fraud that if anything ever happened to my family or me, they would come back and kill him. Nobody would be able to find his body.

Joe and I played golf on that Monday afternoon, Susan, Julie and the girls went shopping, and we came home on Tuesday. I later found out that Hasting Mutual paid the guy $500. Jay said it was a token payment to make him go away—a formality–and how these types of situations are settled.

CHAPTER 16

Transitions at Home

2002

LAURA GRADUATED FROM Garrett Evangelical Seminary in 2002, a few days before Jenna graduated from high school on a Sunday around the end of May. I wasn't on the school board any longer, so I didn't get to give Jenna her diploma like I did Laura and Andrea.

2003

Laura took her first job at the First United Methodist Church in Valparaiso, Indiana. I was overwhelmed with our first church visit. We walked in the door, and people greeted us and made us feel welcome. We went into the sanctuary, and it was beautiful. Laura delivered the message, and when the service was over, the congregation gathered for coffee and doughnuts. *This is the way church services should be,* I thought to myself. I immediately began to figure out how we could do that in our church at home.

2004-2005

The new year arrived, and it was time to check the mailbox for tax forms. Cleon Point was our accountant, and we usually met with him the previous November to plan for the coming year. Cleon was a great man, a former IRS agent who knew the ins and outs of what we could and couldn't deduct. We started doing business with him around 1974 or 1975, and afterward, we met for lunch several times a year as friends.

Susan, me, Andrea, Jenna and Laura in 2003

Cleon taught me how to be a good bookkeeper and put items in the proper categories, so it made life easy for him when he prepared our taxes. I remember once Cleon noticed I had attempted to deduct something that I shouldn't have.

"What do you think you are doing trying to deduct all of your car as a farm car?" he roared.

About this time, his dog, who was always at his side, started barking and growling at me. We didn't know what to think.

"OK, Cleon, do what needs to be done," I said, "just don't let your dog bite me."

I looked to Cleon as my guide to many things in life, and I knew I could use him as a sounding board and he would always be honest with me.

Susan and I picked up our taxes at Cleon's office around February 28, 2004. Cleon and his wife Jan were extremely busy at the end of February, but this day he had time to talk to us. We talked for some time about their children, and he asked about our children. We had great fellowship. What I didn't know was that it would be the last time I saw Cleon alive. A few months later he dropped dead from a heart attack.

I didn't know what to think when I heard the news. One of my best friends and the man I trusted the most for all my financial advice had just passed. I felt deserted and didn't know where to turn. I later met with Jan, and she introduced us to Carl Bergstrom, who had taken over most of Cleon's clients.

My brother-in-law, Stan, my sister, Janet, and their daughter, Brooke (Not pictured, son, Kevin)

I found Carl to be just like Cleon, only he didn't raise his voice as loud when I had something in a wrong category. Carl couldn't believe how organized I was, and I told him that it was Cleon who had taught me. Our family started working with Carl just like we did with Cleon. The only thing missing was Cleon and his dog. I made plans with Carl to meet in November, just like we did with Cleon.

Cleon will always have a special place in my heart, but I had made a new friend in Carl.

Susan and I, along with Joe and Julie Breisch, got tickets for the Indianapolis Colts and Denver Broncos game in Denver on January 2, 2005. We flew out with the Colts fan club, but soon discovered that our tickets were in a high corner of the stadium. After we checked into our hotel, Joe and I headed to the stadium to see if we could get better tickets. The parking lot didn't have a lot of cars in it, and we saw a fellow coming out a side door. He saw us and asked if there was anything he could do to help us.

We told him we had come to town with the Colts fan club to watch the game, but our seats were really high in the corner of the stadium. I explained to him that my wife didn't do well with heights. The gentleman invited Joe and me into the stadium and took us to his office. While we were walking, I noticed a big ring on his finger. We took a seat in his office and visited for about ten minutes before he asked if we had ever seen a Super Bowl ring. It was shiny but a bit too big for my finger.

Mr. Beeler at the farm with his granddaughter and great granddaughter along with Dad, Mom and me

We started talking about tickets, and he said he could help us out but that the only tickets he had were kind of expensive. When he told us the price, Joe and I looked at each other.

"We don't go on vacation very often," I told Joe, "and if you don't tell the girls, I won't either."

Joe and I choked and bought the tickets, and the gentleman showed us where the seats were—they were good. I didn't have to worry about Susan's fear of heights, but we now had eight tickets for four people. Later that evening we went to McCormick and Schmick's Steak and Seafood restaurant, and I asked the waitress if she would trade our meals for the football game tickets that were up pretty high in the stadium. She said she would love to and that, although they were huge Broncos fans, she, her father and brother had never been to a Broncos game.

She went to ask the manager. When he came to the table and saw the delight on the girl's face, he said the restaurant would cover our meals if we would give the tickets to her. Everyone was happy, and Joe and I left the girl an extra large tip.

The next day we drove west through the Eisenhower Tunnel. When we got to the other side of the mountain, we drove into a blizzard. There were vehicles off the road, and it seemed like it took us forever to find a place to turn around and go back the east side of the tunnel. We made it back safely, but the weather forecast said the temperature was going to plummet on game day. We shopped for warmer clothes, which was a good thing because it turned real cold. Joe even bought some heating packets that we put in our gloves and shoes. Those little things saved the day.

We got to the game, and the seats were as good as we had remembered. After the first few plays, the starters for the Colts stayed on the bench. The Colts got blown out that time, but the next week at the playoff game the Colts blew out the Broncos. This was a great trip. It is always nice to take vacations with other people, and when you can find those folks with whom you are compatible, you have real friends.

2006-2007

Jenna graduated from Indiana University in 2006. All of my girls now had college degrees. The only problem was that the girls grew up with Purdue clothes, and I always thought they would go to Purdue. Dad may have been disappointed, but even when parents have plans for their children, they sometimes have to realize that God has bigger plans. I've learned to listen when God is directing, even when it's not what I was expecting.

Laura, Andrea, and Jenna wearing their IU shirts to tease Dad

Jenna moved to Indianapolis on April 2, 2007, to work at VMS BioMarketing. I was really glad that Jenna got the job, but it was still hard to see one of my children move away from home. Jenna could take care of herself, but I had a softer heart than she would ever know.

"Why didn't you cry when you dropped me off at IU the first time like you did when we dropped Laura off at the University of Evansville?" Jenna asked me.

I told her that when the first child goes away for the first time, it is very different than anything a parent has ever experienced in life. Children are the most important creations that parents have in their lives, and they want to protect their children. I prayed to God for the girls' safety every day. As a matter of fact, I believe in praying at any time of the day—mostly silently—and most people don't even know that my personal relationship with God is so precious.

I'm not one to go to the altar or talk much in church, because I want my actions to speak for me by the way I live my life. I am not perfect, and I hope those around me can forgive me for my shortcomings.

I told Jenna that it was an emotional shock when Laura first went to college. I saw her get along and make new friends, and I realized that she was now a young adult and the teachings she had learned growing up were now going to be lived out in real life.

"I didn't cry when we left you off for college because I knew you would be like your sisters," I explained to Jenna. "You were trained well while growing up, and I knew you would make good decisions. I also knew my part was now to pray for you and the other girls' safety."

CHAPTER 17

Saying Goodbye

2008 STARTED LIKE MOST OTHER YEARS. We got the crop planted, and Dad was spending more time in the house but would come out to work some. He seemed to be mellowing out with age, and he wasn't as critical as I had remembered him in the past. He hauled a few loads of corn each day and asked me what I thought about getting a semi tractor with an automatic transmission. I thought it was a great idea, but I really didn't know much about the automatic transmissions in semi tractors.

I have always been partial to Volvo semis, so Dad and I went to General Truck Sales in Muncie, Indiana, to see what they had. They had the perfect semi tractor for hauling grain. It was a 2007, 405-horse Volvo with about 18,000 miles on it. It was in their leasing program but was not leased out at the time. We found out very quickly that we had to purchase the truck outright because they didn't want to give us much in trade for our 1991s and 1995s, and of course, we wouldn't trade our 2004. We bought the truck and brought it home about a week later. That truck was the nicest semi we had ever had.

Laura was ordained as a Methodist minister in the spring. For the girl who, as a junior at the University of Evansville, wasn't sure where she would fit in life, she now had a clear answer. This is a lesson for others to just keep in tune with God, pray to Him, ask for His guidance and wisdom, and He will be there for you. When you do this, you may find He was there to guide you when you didn't even know it.

In the spring we planted our crop and then attended to it by spraying for weeds, insects and fungus. By the end of July, Dad had hauled seven loads with that new truck. Dad had had a pacemaker for several years and later a defibrillator had been added. But on a Monday early in August he had a heart attack. They had to shock him in the ambulance going to the hospital, and he eventually ended up at St. Vincent where Dr. Reardon, his heart doctor, practiced.

Dad and Mom

The prognosis wasn't good. Dad was struggling. He couldn't keep food down, and he made it clear he didn't want to be shocked again. Dad called me over to the bed and said he wanted them to turn off his defibrillator because he wasn't going to get any better. He wanted me to make sure that everyone knew it was his choice to disconnect it. Dad then said we needed to make some farm changes fairly quickly.

I immediately called our attorney, Tom Trauring. His paralegal answered the phone, and I explained why I was calling. Tom asked specific questions. He inquired if I knew what the will said, and I stated I did not. I said I thought I had a copy in the lock box, but it was sealed, and I was never given permission to look at it. Tom told me what was in the will. I knew I was the executor, but I talked to Dad about removing Key Bank as the trustee and adding Carl Bergstrom. He felt much better because he knew he could trust Carl.

Dr. Reardon came to Dad's room to confirm that Dad still wanted to be disconnected from the defibrillator, and he said yes. After disconnecting the defibrillator, Dr. Reardon came out of Dad's room with tears in his eyes and said my father's wishes had been granted. It was a sad and difficult moment. Dad's condition was stable, but the next time his heart went out of rhythm he would pass away.

It was decided the hospital had done all it could do, and together we worked it out with Century Villa to put Dad into the rehab section. I rode in the ambulance with Dad. He felt every bump we hit, and I felt so bad for him, but there was nothing anyone could do. We made it to Greentown, and the workers at Century Villa had Dad's room ready. They were very nice to my father. He'd been there about three days when the nurse in charge called me to her office.

She asked me if I knew how bad my father was. I told her I thought I did. She said from his blood work that he should not even be alive. She had never seen anyone with blood work like his who was as solid in his mind as he was—not to mention breathing on his own. Dad did not have the strength to walk, move or even sit up. His mind was solid, but his body was worn out.

Laura and Daniel McMasters were married on August 9. The wedding was at the Grace United Methodist Church in Kokomo, and the reception was at PASTArrific. Laura and Daniel had a morning wedding, so their out-of-state friends would be able to arrive back home at a decent time. They had several friends from Tennessee at the wedding, including the president and vice president of the college where they worked.

The wedding was great, but Dad being so sick made it tough mentally for me. The wedding pictures were taken without Dad, and I wanted to try to crop him into the photos some way, but it didn't happen.

I really just wanted my dad to be well enough to be at the wedding. As soon as the reception was over, Laura and Daniel went to Century Villa to see him.

On August 17, we were in the middle of a family lunch at our home when Dr. Sedaghat called me on my cell phone and told us to get to Century Villa as soon as possible. We immediately headed there, and I called Joe and Julie Breisch on the way to Greentown. Julie is a nurse and met us at Dad's room.

"He can still hear you," she said, "but he is on his last breaths."

Dad took three short breaths a few seconds apart and slipped away. My mother, sister and I made funeral arrangements the next day. I still can't believe all the people who showed up for my dad's calling. We had it at our church, First United Methodist Church of Greentown.

There are specific things one remembers at times like this. Sonny and Glendia Beck were the first ones at the door for the calling. Landlords that I very seldom see showed up for the funeral. Tom Trauring, our attorney, came to the funeral and the calling. These are special moments when people you don't expect show up. Not least, but last was my good friend from Pulaski, Tennessee, Bartt McCormack, who walked in the church door just minutes before the funeral was to start.

The service was really special, with our oldest daughter, Pastor Laura, presiding. Our nephew, Father Kevin Middlesworth, spoke as well, and every grandchild had a part in the service. Pastor Michael Goodspeed officiated, but the grandchildren performed the service. At the cemetery, I had a picture of all the family members and employees imprinted on the top of the casket. That moment didn't last long, but that memory has lasted forever. I performed the military rites for my father, and the American Legion Post 317 saluted him.

The services were over, and everyone had gone back home, when Mom said she didn't want to live on the farm without Dad. We proceeded to get her an apartment at Century Fields. Her health was failing, but she was still able to drive. She loved ice cream, and she brought it to the field on my birthday for all the employees. These are examples of some of the priceless moments we had with her.

This picture is one of the times Mom brought ice cream to the field on my birthday.

I, on the other hand, had issues to deal with. Every time I went somewhere Dad and I had been, I lost it. It was tough. When I went to the barn the first time, knowing Dad would never be back,

I couldn't help but cry. I soon learned that each time I had one of these moments, it was best to just let the tears flow and not try to stop them until I was cried out. Time does heal. The thoughts and sadness never go away, but time allows one to accept life as it really is. We are on earth for a short time, I remind myself. How do I want to be remembered?

It is amazing what all has to be done when someone passes. You have to get a death certificate to open an estate. Then, several months later, after the state and federal governments—and in some cases family—are all satisfied, the estate is closed. Going through the entire process has caused me to be more clear in my will and to have a very detailed successor plan.

I had farmed my entire life with my father. Dad and I didn't always tell Mom everything because she would sometimes let it slip to her friends or maybe just didn't hear the story correctly. If we bought a combine, tractor, piece of farm equipment or even a farm, we told her after the fact. Mom was very conservative. We would try to talk her into getting new clothes, but she just didn't have the will to be flashy. If Susan or Janet took her to town, that was a different story. If they said it looked good, then it was OK to purchase.

Mom got settled in to Century Fields in November after Dad passed. For a while, she went back to the farm during the daytime. She was like the queen bee while she was healthy, and she visited many people who were in the nursing home. We picked her up for church almost every Sunday and then went to my favorite place to eat afterward—PASTArrific in Kokomo, Indiana.

CHAPTER 18

Moving Forward

W E HAD TO GET ALL THE LAND that Dad had in his name or shared with me or mom appraised. While doing this, I had specific parcels appraised, so Mom and I could trade land and have me end up with the farmstead that I already owned half interest in.

I wanted to move to the farm, but Susan did not. The electric company was going to take the farm off residential rate and put us on commercial by demand. This would have been very expensive compared to what the electric bill had always been, so I negotiated with the electric company to keep the residential rate, but we had to move there. I explained this to Susan, but she still did not want to move.

After approaching her the third time in about a 10-day period, I asked her if she was moving with me. She just started crying. We had our home on 200 South remodeled just like she wanted it. It was difficult for her to give that up. It was also paid in full. If we moved, we could continue to use the old house as an office and build an attached home to the east. She was still not buying into the proposal.

A few weeks later we were in Tom Trauring's office regarding updating our wills along with business for my dad's estate. I asked Tom if he knew of an architect. He said he could get us a good one. Susan spoke up and said, "If you're going to get an architect, then it is OK to build and move." By the time we could get everything put together, we weren't able to start building until April 15, 2010.

2009

Early in 2009, Susan and I took Mom back to their home in Florida so she could see her friends. I never told her, but with the feelings I had going to the places where Dad and I had gone together in the past, it was important to me. It brought back memories that would help heal. You could tell Mom's friends at Braden Castle really cared for her. In the past few years, they were at her side when she had a heart attack and a knee replacement.

After coming home from Bradenton, we concentrated on preparing the ground surface for the new fuel station. I had all the land and farm equipment appraised, and I spent a lot of time in the attorney's office trying to help him understand the complex estate. I had already owned half of the farm equipment before Dad died. He had wanted me to buy his half out the year before. At that time, I had had everything appraised, and then the conversation was dropped. I was afraid to bring it back up because I didn't want to upset him. It most likely would have cost me less than after he passed.

2010-2011

2010 was a very busy year for Susan and me. We finally started to build the house. The project was very interesting, but I don't want to do it again. Susan and I had picked out a brick that we liked, but she wanted some stone to kind of mix in with the brick. We decided to go to Wisconsin where different kinds of stone were being dug. We went to the quarry and Susan found the stone right away. We told them how much we wanted, when we wanted it and where to deliver it. Susan was very pleased. We moved into the house on December 21, 2010.

2011 started with a big bang. On January 2, at 7:55 a.m., I was working in my office, Susan was taking a shower in the basement and a big bang and shaking began. It lasted 10 to 15 seconds. (The records say it was December 10, 2010, but I'm not sure about that.) My toy tractors and semis on my overhead cabinets were rolling.

I checked on Susan, and she was OK. I went outside to see if our two 12,000-gallon LP tanks had blown up. I then looked all around to see if a plane had crashed. A few minutes later Jay called and asked if we were OK. I told him we were, but something had really shaken the house. He told me we had just had an earthquake very close to us. I told him that, the way the place shook, it had to be close. The earthquake was originally measured at a 4.2 on the Richter scale but later downgraded to a 3.8. The epicenter was about one and one-quarter to one and one-half miles west-southwest of our home. Plaster in the corners of the walls separated, and I went out to the north end of the shop and noticed the cement was cracked. This was my third earthquake experience.

Years earlier, Dad and I had been picking up rocks on the Doyle and Janice David farm, and a pile of rocks just started shaking. I could feel the vibration in the ground. I think that earthquake was in Illinois. The other earthquake was in the Cayman Islands. I was sleeping in that morning when my bed started shaking. I thought it was Terry Keiffer shaking my bed to get me up. A little bit later it shook hard again. I told Terry I would get up, but it wasn't Terry. I got up, and everyone was outside standing and talking. I asked what was going on. They told me we had experienced an earthquake. Sure enough, Terry was outside with the other people.

In the summer of 2011, we remodeled some existing grain bins, built two new bins for soybeans and changed the existing three-phase power to 480. I also continued to work with Tom Trauring on Dad's estate and trading land around so that there would only be one owner per land parcel. I also traded land, so the same owner's land was located in one geographical area and not spread out. This took some time because of the appraisals, but we got it. I knew this would make the transition easier when Mom came to the end of her life, and it did.

Around February we learned that Laura and Daniel were expecting. Everyone was very happy for them. They'd had a miscarriage the year before. We proceeded optimistically, but losing the first child still remained in our minds. Laura was due in September, and Susan and I made our plans to be in Pulaski when our first grandchild came. On September 19, 2011, Susan and I were at the hospital in Columbia, Tennessee, along with Daniel, Laura, Andrea and Daniel's parents. Little Sophia came that morning, and our lives have been changed ever since.

CHAPTER 19

Losing and Gaining

W E COMBATTED A DROUGHT IN 2011, and it was the worst corn crop year we had experienced since 1983. Amazingly, it was also the first time in about 15 years I had federal crop insurance. The premiums are very high. With the expenses farmers have, it is comforting to know insurance is available. I worked with an adjuster from Thanksgiving 2011 until February 2012 substantiating the records. I had scales tickets and the most accurate records he had ever seen.

I had to prove I was telling the truth, and they take the approach the farmers are guilty until proven innocent. This is one of those times in life that you have to be polite, courteous and respectful to the adjuster, or it may cost you dearly in the end. The adjuster lived in Iowa, and we did all communications by voice phone. I scanned the documents that he wanted for each year, and then I had to explain them to him. The documents were self-explanatory, but we had to go through the process. He did everything he could to find something wrong, but he never did. In the end, the 2011 corn crop was not good, but we had a really good soybean crop, which help offset the corn crop.

When you are looking at your fields throughout the summer and seeing corn that did not pollinate well and wondering if you are going to get any rain to develop the soybeans, it is challenging.

You wonder in your mind if you will have enough income to pay the farm rent, fertilizer bills and other payments. A person shouldn't worry about situations in life that they can't control, like the weather for example. It is natural to be concerned, but when these challenges happen, you have to decide you are going to beat the challenge. You must ask God to guide you, direct you and give you the strength to make choices that will be best for your family.

Mom got to see her great granddaughter Sophia that Thanksgiving and a few days after Christmas. Mom was so weak that we had to help hold her head up for the picture. She had gone downhill health-wise and wasn't mobile. They lifted her out of bed with a hoist. She jokingly told me once I needed to take a ride in the hoist just to see what it was like.

"No, thanks, Mom," I told her. "You're doing a good job."

Susan and I had an opportunity to go to the Dominican Republic with Beck's Hybrids the last week in February. We were having a great time, but all I could think of was Mom. On the evening of February 29, 2012, I received an emergency phone call while we were with friends in a restaurant. Mom had passed. My sister said she had a little trouble, and the nurse had left the room. When she came back, it was like she had gone to sleep for the last time.

Scott Beck was near, and I told him about the call.

"We will get you home," he told me, and the next morning we were on the Beck's Hybrids private jet headed for Indianapolis. The following morning I met with my sister and the local funeral home director. Like with Dad we had the calling and the funeral in the First United Methodist Church. Laura was the organizer. Kevin, Andrea, Jenna, and Brooke Chapman all had parts in the service. The grandchildren did great, and it surprised me that some of the things the girls said made everyone laugh. My sister put slides together for people to view while waiting.

When Mom and Dad passed I was amazed at how many people came to the calling and to the funeral. Some you expected to see or hear from, but it was the people you didn't expect to see who brought the tears. We live in a great community, and we should be thankful. People were so kind to our family, and I can't thank them enough for their kindness to us. These are the thoughtful moments you remember for the rest of your life. In life, you are judged by what you do and say. When you pray, always ask God to continue to guide you to make sure the things you think, do and say are pleasing to Him. He will help you have a positive attitude as well.

When Mom passed, we started all over with the business matters that had to happen when someone passes. Wilda Ruth Kirkpatrick became the Wilda Kirkpatrick Estate. Being the executor of Dad's and Mom's estates, I knew what needed to be done. Along with our attorney, Tom Trauring, and our accountant, Carl Bergstrom, we worked on these issues for the rest of the year.

While we were spending a lot of time gathering information for mom's estate, another drought was brewing. Our crops had grown well through the summer, considering the heat and stress they endured. However, both the ears and the corn rows themselves were not fully filled out due to it being too hot to pollinate. When scouting the fields in the last week of July and the first week in August, I knew we were in trouble yield-wise. Not to mention the soybeans which were hanging in there just waiting for a rain.

The 2012 corn crop was similar to 2011—not good. We had farmed all these years and had seen nothing this bad since 1983 and 1988, with 1983 being my worst corn crop ever. The 2012 soybeans did get a little rain starting the first week of August. Those little rains just kept coming. Each time it rained, more blooms would come and more pods would set. It was truly a blessing. We had the best soybeans in my history of farming.

Jenna worked for VMS in Indianapolis and had decided she wanted more out of life, so she applied to the University of Michigan to earn a masters degree in business administration. After earning her degree, she was hired by Chrysler Corporation in Auburn Hills, Michigan. Since working at Chrysler, she has traveled promoting the Dodge Charger and other vehicles. She also has had other opportunities at Chrysler. This was another instance in which Jenna had a passion to do more in life, and God directed her and showed her the way to nurture that passion.

On July 21, 2012, Andrea married Doug Lantz. They were married at their home. It was a rather informal wedding with a cowboy theme and a lot of really good food. Andrea and Doug were married by Andrea's sister, Pastor Laura McMasters. During the reception, they had each of their attendants roast them instead of toast them. It created funny memories to last a lifetime.

As 2012 came to an end, all the family gathered at our house for Thanksgiving. It would have been a repeat performance in December, but the McMasters were not able to come for Christmas. Laura, Daniel and Sophia celebrated instead with Daniel's family in Loretto, Tennessee.

CHAPTER 20

Blessed

2013

I HAVE SOLD BECK'S SUPERIOR HYBRIDS seed since 1976. If customers pay their bills by certain dates they can get cash discounts. One of those dates is the tenth of January each year. The payment due is 10 percent. If a customer's seed bill is $300,000, then his cash discount equals $30,000. Susan and I always stay around home through the first few weeks of January, as it is important for us to be available when my customers want to pay.

In 2013, we had an opportunity to go to the Cayman Islands with three other customers—a great way to start a new year. We had a few customers who wanted the 10 percent cash discount, so I worked with them while I was in Cayman. I've learned I can be away from home and still take care of business. I sign into my home office computer from wherever I am in the world. I knew talking on the phone in Cayman was very expensive, but I was able to have a vacation and continue with office work as usual.

If it were not for our employees who carry on the day-to-day outside operations, this would have been impossible. Kevin Breisch, Gerald Miller, Tom Dickover, Joe Breisch, and Kevin

Moss take care of the outside operations for the most part, and we have more part-time help in the spring and fall.

Beck's hosted another trip to the Panama Canal in early February. We learned a lot about the history of the Panama Canal, the people and the French and US militaries who finally finished the canal that France had started. We also drove by the prison where General Noriega is a permanent guest.

I knew of General Noriega from history. When Laura was at Garrett Evangelical Seminary and Andrea was at Kendall College next door, Danny Huston asked if I would go with him to Chicago for some business. On the same trip, I could stop by and see the girls. I said I would.

Danny was going to his new partner's home to prepare for a speech that he had to give later in the year. While Danny practiced with a speech instructor, Jeff (of previous Chicago fame) and I looked over his guns. Jeff handed me a revolver, and it had General Noriega's name engraved on it. It was one of the former Navy SEALs that teach at Jeff's facility that had captured General Noriega and given Jeff the revolver that General Noriega had on him the day he was captured.

After looking at the revolver, Jeff took a phone call. He and his wife, Patty, were both on the line, when she started crying. One of their Navy SEALs friends had passed away. Jeff told me later that that SEAL alone had 70 very sensitive missions for the CIA. This farmer had a rude awakening to the real world that day.

When the harvest was over, we went to Jenna and Greer's in Detroit. While Jenna works for Chrysler, Greer Love works for Huron Capital Partners. Jenna had met him through her Indiana University friends. She had gotten engaged to Greer on Memorial Day weekend, and they planned the wedding for July of the next year.

All the family was home for Christmas that year except Greer. We had Christmas at Susan's parents' as we do every year on Christmas Eve and left there in time to attend the Christmas Eve service at our church at 9:00 p.m. The holidays go fast, everyone goes home and then the house is quiet compared to when all the family is there. That is what life is all about. You work your rear end off throughout the year and then enjoy every holiday with family and friends. In the middle of working hard, remember to play hard as well. Visit, rest and just enjoy family and friends.

2014

The 2013 harvest was over and we didn't have to deal with the federal crop insurance adjusters. What we did have to deal with was the price of corn. It had fallen so low that the profits weren't like they had been the previous two years. Those profits had allowed us to bump up our cash rent to the landowners and give them huge bonuses. When putting the farm plan together for the 2014 crop, I realized the expenses were not going to come down enough to keep paying the landlords the same amount of cash rent.

Aerial view of our home and farm

It is hard to ask landlords to accept less cash rent when they have become accustomed to the larger payments. My farm plan included all expenses for every product expected to be used on every acre of our farm, as well as the total projected cost. Included in this scenario is always the reapplication of the fertilizer taken off the field from the previous crop. I like to replace and add a little as a precaution. It is important that the fertilizer and lime be applied accurately to the soil by using GPS. This is part of being an ethical farmer who recognizes the importance of being a good steward of the soil—which is essential for generations to come. It is hard for me to accept the concept of farmers who go out and bid high-cash rent for a farm and then strip the soil of the nutrients that the previous farmer put in the soil, and not replace them.

In June of the previous year, Susan and I had been able to purchase the farmland around the house I grew up in. I had stated that if I ever owned that, one day I would tear all the old buildings down and build a condo for Susan's John Deere equipment. That dream came true in 2014.

Andrea and Doug were about to have their first child—Susan's and my second grandchild. Josslyn Elena Lantz was born on March 31, 2014. When parents and grandparents are blessed with new life, it is like a miracle. Joss has been a great joy and is a perfect match with our first granddaughter, Sophia. It has been great watching these girls as they grow.

Jenna and Greer were married July 27, 2014, in Detroit, Michigan, in the Detroit Athletic Club by Jenna's sister, Pastor Laura McMasters. The guests were their immediate family members along with a few very close friends. Greer's stepfather and mother, Mike and Kathy, hosted a beautiful evening meal the night before. They gave great speeches, and all I could think of was what I was going to say at the wedding reception. Mike and Kathy had their speeches written out, and I had nothing prepared.

Jenna had asked me long before if I would make a speech at the reception, but I hadn't thought it was necessary to prepare. After Mike and Kathy finished, I thought to myself that I should have been working on a speech instead of spending my time at the GM Center and the boardwalk the two previous days. At any rate, I took a little time and asked God to help me say the right words at the reception. I wrote down a few thoughts that evening and the next morning.

After the wedding, we ate hors d'oeuvres before moving into the dining hall for dinner. Andrea was asked to say a few words, and of course, she did a great job and had everyone laughing. I, in the meantime, still didn't have a concrete speech. I reviewed my five line items to make sure I would get them into the speech. I prayed, "Lord, I need your help now." At that moment I knew this was a time to speak from my heart and not to worry about a prepared speech. I thank God for guiding me.

During one of my most pleasant moments, I mentioned my parents and Greer's father who were deceased. This hit home hard, but it came out of love and respect for them and what they had taught us. I don't think that was one of the five sentences that I had prepared. It felt like I spoke for a long time. God helped me along the way to help my choice of words be meaningful.

On one of my walks to the GM Center, a man and woman approached and proceeded to corner me on the street. The woman was on my right side, and the man was on my left. They moved in very close, as though they were going to grab me. They then asked me for money. I told them I was from Indiana and was trying to get a ride back to Indiana. They still wanted to know if I would give them some cash, so I emptied my pockets and explained I didn't have any.

The woman left my side and crossed the street, but the man stayed right with me. He started telling me about his life and how he wished he could have changed it. We talked about God for a while before he went his way and I went mine. The next morning, as Daniel, Laura's husband, and I walked back to the GM Center, we ran into the man and woman again. I immediately told them that I had found my ride back to Indiana. He said, "God bless you," and I said, "May God be with you always; never give up, and I will keep praying to Him to help you."

Each year we travel to Tennessee to celebrate our granddaughter Sophia's birthday. That year was her third birthday party. We came back from Tennessee, and it was time to start harvest. We harvested the highest yielding corn crop ever on our farm and the second highest soybean crop.

The only problem was the price of corn had dropped below production costs. This made it very difficult to meet our expenses, and I immediately put a freeze on all spending. That didn't work well. Due to the rainy fall, I felt it necessary to buy a third combine to harvest soybeans. I also upgraded the 1,000-bushel grain cart to another 1,500-bushel grain cart on tracks. This was one of those years that we had to be in the field whenever the weather was right for harvesting.

We finished harvest on November 5, and if it weren't for the third combine, it most likely would have been Thanksgiving or later. What was even worse, I had built a 270-foot by 98-foot tool shed. I'd signed the purchase order when corn was $5 per bushel, and by the time it was built, the corn price was down to $3.40 per bushel. So much for a spending freeze!

Susan and I are so fortunate to have the great employees that we have. They all work together, and they know what needs to be done without being micromanaged. We apply the strengths of each person to their role on the farm. God has blessed us, I am confident He will continue to bless us, and I hope God feels we are faithful to Him.

CHAPTER 21

A Family Affair

WHEN IT COMES TO RELIGION, I have accepted Jesus Christ as my personal Savior. I am not always a perfect person, but I do ask forgiveness when I sin. Each of us has our own weaknesses in life, and that is why it is so important to choose a church where you will hear, study and share the word of God. Hopefully, this will help each of us to be a better person. I ask for forgiveness and for God to help me. If I don't pause in situations that provoke me, I will get drawn in. Put a stop to immediate comebacks when put in this situation. Think about what was said, and either don't say anything or reply respectfully—whether serious or teasing.

In November 2014, Susan, Andrea, Doug, Joss, Doug's parents, Greer's parents, sister and brother-in-law went to Greer and Jenna's for Thanksgiving. We had a great time. We ate brunch at the Detroit Athletic Club, and Greer took the guys to the Lions and Bears game. As the end of 2014 drew near, all the children and grandchildren visited our home. We had a memorable Christmas, and we thanked God for this wonderful blessing. We continually thank Him for our family and friends and most of all for His Son who died on the cross that we may have eternal life.

After Christmas and before the New Year, it was now time to pay year-end bills and work on the 2015 farm plan. I hoped 2015 didn't end up like 2009. That year, the price of fertilizer had been high, and the price of grain had fallen even lower than usual.

2015

Now it's 2015—January 3, to be exact. While the guys work outside, I try to finish the crop plan regarding expenses to put the crop out. Adam, my agronomist, and I agreed to prices on December 29, 2014. Now I have to bill the products that go on each field. This will tell me the total amounts of each product that I need to purchase and what my expenses are.

I have just finished inputting all the information on my EASi Suites program. I began using Easy Crops software program in the 1980s and then switched to EASi Suites in the 90s. Prior to EASi Suites, I used basic spreadsheets, Datastar and Reportstar. Nowadays, all of my farming records are in EASi Suites and my financial records are recorded in a program called CenterPoint by Red Wing software. And to think, I started out years ago with paper ledger books!

I am always running projections regarding predicted income and expenses. 2015 and 2016 look grim. We had high corn and soybean yields in 2014 coupled with the lowest prices since 2008-2010. Add to that the highest expenses ever to put out the crops. When prices went to $7.82 on corn in the droughts of 2011 and 2012 we made more profit with the drought than with a large crop. My 2015 projections do not look promising. If grain prices keep going down, it could become a serious situation for agricultural communities. I have been in contact with my landlords, and they know the farm economy is not thriving.

I will keep running projections and hope the farm economy doesn't continue the downslide. The risks farmers take when putting out a crop are more than most people can ever imagine. We have no control of fertilizer, seed and all other input costs to put out a crop. This also includes the economy of other countries who buy our grain. The value of the US dollar has an effect on whether or not other countries can buy US grains at the cheapest price. We have no control of the price we get for our grain produced. We hope to find the right price and time to market our grain, which is not so easy. We also have to keep an eye on stored grain so that it doesn't get hot and spoil. We hope the prices get high enough that they will give us a profit.

On this January evening, Susan, Phil and Jane Gentis and I are going to the Purdue vs. Michigan basketball game. Mr. Beck has given us very good seats in the TV section. We have to wear Purdue colors to sit here, and the chairs are really nice in this section.

As I am getting ready to go to the game, I can't help but think about what my cousin Phil has gone through in the last year and a half. His brother, Gene, died and Gene's wife had no services for him. Gene's children were on their way to Kentucky where he lived, and he was gone before they got there. The day he passed, Phil, David Arrendale and I were at the Indianapolis Motor Speedway for the Nascar events on Friday prior to the race on Sunday. Phil, Dave and I were making plans to see Phil's brother in Kentucky who has been ill. We were walking back to the Beck suite in front of where the race drivers park their motor homes, and Phil said he had gotten a text, but he couldn't read it. He asked me what is said. I read it to him. It said his brother Gene had passed. It was a rough few moments.

Then, his mother died at the end of 2014. My sister and I are the closest relatives on his father's side of the family that Phil has. Regarding immediate family, I have my wife, children, grandchildren and a sister left while Phil only has his wife, children and grandchildren. This is a feeling that sometimes is hard to cope with. We feel Gene was taken way too soon, and to make things worse there has not been a funeral for Gene. He was cremated immediately. I always will wonder why his wife didn't have a funeral or a memorial for Gene out of the respect for his family. In my opinion, there are too many unanswered questions regarding Gene's death. They'll probably stay unanswered.

It's now January 7. I have been studying the three 2014 Farm Bill Choices for the new program that will last 2014-2018. The USDA is a little behind if it makes farmers go into a new program without having put all the facts in easy terms for the farmers to understand. If it weren't for the professors at Purdue University, University of Illinois, Iowa and Texas, the farmers still might not understand the new bill.

MARCH 2015

It is now March 2015 and I am working on some fair projects. I have been chairman of the Fair Planning Committee for a long time. We are building a new restroom at the fairgrounds near the round barn. It will be built to fit in with the Pioneer Village theme. As soon as we get the drawings from the architect, we will call a fair planning committee meeting, so together we can choose a contractor. We will also discuss some other maintenance issues on the fair grounds. Danny Huston, of North American Midway, has offered to pay half of the cost of paving our midway. We have the specs but need approval from the fair planning committee to proceed. Then we will need the approval of the fair board. Final approval will be determined by a vote of the members of the Greentown Lions Club.

At the farm, both excavators and the dozer are down south of the creek where I am leveling the dirt off from when it was dredged years ago. When the creek was dredged there were a lot of rocks and sand that came out and were put on top of good native soil. The dump truck hauled most of it to my boyhood farm last summer. I needed the dredged dirt to raise the elevation of the new toolshed high enough that water wouldn't run in it. At any rate I am trying to level the area off south of the creek to get down to the native soil that was at the surface before the creek dirt was deposited on top of it. I figure if I can move the dirt that remains to the edge of the bank and taper it down about 20 feet I can pick up about 2 acres of original native farm land.

Susan and my mother used to run the tractors, plow, rip ground, drive semis and operate our grain carts. While doing this, our younger children sat in baby seats right next to them. Those were the best days of farming. My father, Robert, my mother, Wilda, my wife Susan, Tom Dickover and Kevin Moss (part-time) ran the farm.

I have been talking to my Beck's District Sales Manager, Kyle, about the Beck's 300-Bushel Challenge. I told him if I entered a plot for myself then I wanted to enter a plot for Susan, too. Kyle said he would make that happen. I chose 30 acres that Susan and I own together for her and another 30 acres that I own for me. The parcel that Susan has was a portion of the field that I won the Junior Howard County corn yield contest on years ago. (A while back we installed system drain tiling in these fields.) I chose Beck's hybrid 5509A3 for Susan and 5828AMX for myself. Two ounces of Stratego and Evergreen were applied to both fields as a foliar feed along with our normal fertilizing program. The foliar feed program was applied around V5 to V8. (A V5 is when 5 leaves are showing with what looks like a collar under the leaves.)

***

Our farm is a family farm. My wife, Susan, works on it just like our employees and I do. Every person on the farm has a role to play. Even my girls and their husbands are part of the plans and operations of our farm. When the girls were small, they ran tractors working ground and walked soybeans pulling weeds. I want people to understand that besides running a combine or a tractor there are other crucial responsibilities. For instance, Susan, Andrea and Janice cook for the help, pay routine bills, make quick trips to get parts, fill driving semis, sometimes act as weigh master, mow our and a few landlords' yards, be on call for the unexpected and much more.

From the very beginning, I've had a feeling Susan was going to beat me. I've even been hoping she would. We just received the 2014 results for Beck's 300 Bushel Challenge. Susan had the highest corn yield in Indiana at 267.4 bushels per acre. She was 14th overall in Beck's marketing area which includes Indiana, Kentucky, Illinois, Ohio, Michigan and Tennessee. I had to include Tennessee so I could tell my good friend Bartt McCormack that my wife beat him in this challenge. I was third in Indiana at 264.3 bushels per acre and 16th overall in this contest.

It is my opinion that no other occupation can give a person that same joy in life as working on a farm with your family members and friends. Today, Susan, Andrea and Janice are super busy fixing lunch and supper for our employees. When we are not in the fields or trucking, we have lunch in the farm kitchen. Working in the fields means lunch and supper are packed in coolers for all 13 workers.

There is nothing better than to be out in a field on a tractor or a combine enjoying the view of God's creation. I spend a lot of time praying to God and feeling His peace and love there. This is always a great feeling. Unfortunately, it seems like it's when I'm in this deep feeling that something always breaks on the equipment, and I have to come back to reality.

CHAPTER 22

Final Thoughts

A S I HAVE SAID BEFORE, IN WHATEVER WE DO, I pray to God to help us meet new friends and expand our realm of knowledge. I pray that we are kept safe and we don't cause harm to our fellow man.

I have attended church since I was born. My parents taught me how important it was to have a church family. As I look back and even today my church family has been and always will be very important to me becoming a better person in life. They will be there in time of need, they will also share in joys and sorrows that we go through in life. The church family is always there. God works through each of us, and His love never ends.

I have tried to write my true story from the time I can actually remember life. There has been much joy and sadness. Each time our church family was always there for us. I hope you understand that by attending church you will find people who you can share your friendship with. Going to church is to worship God, but you get more out of life by visiting and working with your friends that you have made. Keep those friends forever.

In 1991, when my wife and I decided to attend the First United Methodist Church of Greentown, we met a lot of new friends. One person in particular was Joe Breisch. We immediately talked about the late '60s, and we became close friends. There are more examples of my church friends we met who still mean a lot to us today. We found them by attending church, becoming involved and letting Christ guide the way.

Joe Breisch and Bryan Kirkpatrick in 2015

I have also been the lay leader of the First United Methodist Church in Greentown, Indiana, for the last several years. When working with other people we must keep in mind that people have different personalities, have been raised in different lifestyles, and may have had experiences that mold their attitudes. That is why some people may have different opinions about certain subjects or issues, when they are discussed. At times someone will express an opinion that sometimes catches people off guard. Having different opinions on issues is sometimes good. There are times when one has to go out of his comfort zone and listen to an opinion that is outside the box so to speak. This is another time when I say, "Nothing can be a thing until it was once a thought." We must always respect the thoughts of other people. When God gets involved, one of those thoughts will most likely become a thing and be very productive.

There are leaders and followers in the realm of life. There may be trying times once in a while, but if you ask God for His help, He will be there. Remember to be patient with God. True friends know the real feelings of their friend's heart, and that is one of the many reasons being on God's team is so special. It is important to show Christian love for each other. There are many people in need, and sometimes that need is for someone to ask, "How are you today?" You can do outreach ministry by being kind to all people that you associate with. Let your friends know you care for them by showing kindness at all times. The best thing that anyone can do for their fellow man is to "Treat everyone you come in contact with like you would want to be treated yourself." That is kind of what God does for us by working through each of us when we may not even know it. That is also His Golden Rule.

Everyday each of us faces challenges. Some are not so difficult, while others are arduous. The best way to meet all challenges is to ask God to help you. The longer you wait to ask God for guidance, the longer it will take before you have peace in your heart. If you ask, He will not let you down. This is one of the gifts that you can receive by accepting Jesus Christ as your personal Savior. He will always be there for you. Sometimes we have to be more patient than we want to be. He will help often when you don't even know He is. I know you will be in prayerful thought with Him, listen to Him and be thankful as I will.

I want to talk about spiritual gifts that you have been born with. You may not realize you have certain gifts. I urge you to take time to look in the mirror and look yourself in the eyes and ask yourself, "What do I do best in my life? What comes natural for me? What do I do best in my life that is productive in the lifecycle?" Realize that people do not have the same gifts. That is what makes the world go 'round, so to speak. Be thankful for people possessing gifts that you don't have, and be sure to use the gifts God has given you effectively. If all the people in a church, an organization, or a business utilized their gifts and were willing to listen and share thoughts with each other, they would be successful.

Today is April 2, 2015. We are ready to start planting but waiting on the weather. We have no idea what the farm season will be like this year. I can tell you that I will leave it up to God.

We have two employees taking trees out of fence rows, one employee trucking seed from Beck's to our seed shed, one loading seed out of the seed shed onto customer trailers, and two cooking lunch and making sure the checkbook is balanced correctly. Our middle daughter, Andrea, will be home, and I plan to teach her how to do inputs on every field, record grain deliveries and keep inventories correctly. Another employee and I will be doing charity for the Greentown Lions Club dba Howard County 4-H Fair. We have other employees that work part-time.

I want you to know each person I have mentioned has special gifts that they were born with or taught or that they learned throughout life. They utilize these gifts. Not everyone is a farmer, but everyone has special gifts from God. I ask that you take a look at your special gifts and see how can you apply them in your church and other organizations that serve the community, mankind, and your family. Then, say to yourself that you are blessed. Be thankful and continue to keep in tune with God. I'm sure you will have many more blessings and will be able to pass them on to others.

God has blessed me with a great wife, three daughters, two grandchildren so far, a wonderful church family and great friends all around me. That is what life is all about. Treat others as you would like to be treated, and you will be blessed in your own heart.

People are born at the right time according to God's plan. I was born at a time so that when I was old enough to farm everything fell into place. The implement dealer my dad traded with rented his family farm to me in 1969, my first school teacher and her husband in 1970, and the neighbor across the road in 1971. Several members of our church were retiring, and I was born at the right time and in the right place to get my start in life. I trust God and ask Him to guide me, help me be patient for His plan and give me the wisdom to make the right choices in life. He's had a plan for me, and I thank Him for the many blessings He has given me since my birth.

May God bless each of you who have read this book. I have written from my heart. I hope this story will help you in your life. Take the same approach in life, and share what I have shared with you to others.

God has been good to my family and me, and I hope our friends feel that we share that same kind of love and goodness with them.

CPSIA information can be obtained
at www.ICGtesting.com
Printed in the USA
FFOW05n1726071115

9 781943 294251